THE QUALITIES OF A MASTER TEACHER TODAY

THE QUALITIES OF A MASTER TEACHER TODAY

What's Essential in Reaching All Students

Randall G. Glading

Foreword by Bruce S. Cooper

ROWMAN & LITTLEFIELD
Lanham • Boulder • New York • London

Published by Rowman & Littlefield
A wholly owned subsidiary of The Rowman & Littlefield Publishing Group, Inc.
4501 Forbes Boulevard, Suite 200, Lanham, Maryland 20706
www.rowman.com

Unit A, Whitacre Mews, 26-34 Stannary Street, London SE11 4AB

British Library Cataloguing in Publication Information Available

Library of Congress Cataloging-in-Publication Data

Names: Glading, Randall G., 1955– author.
Title: The qualities of a master teacher today : what's essential in reaching all students / Randall G. Glading.
Description: Lanham : Rowman & Littlefield, [2017] | Includes bibliographical references.
Identifiers: LCCN 2016052919 (print) | LCCN 2017000529 (ebook) | ISBN 9781475835267 (cloth : alk. paper) | ISBN 9781475835274 (pbk. : alk. paper) | ISBN 9781475835281 (electronic)
Subjects: LCSH: Effective teaching.
Classification: LCC LB1025.3 .G5135 2017 (print) | LCC LB1025.3 (ebook) | DDC 371.102—dc23 LC record available at https://lccn.loc.gov/2016052919

Printed in the United States of America

CONTENTS

CONTENTS

FOREWORD

Teachers are vital to our children, their families, and our very society—and so is this book! It extols teachers and their true professional lives, explaining their importance to everyone, including our current and future children and their parents—and how teachers can affect their lives and well-being. Hence, Randall Glading, gladly, begins by awakening us and reminding us of our own personal "memories" and "recollections" of great teachers and teaching—and also, sadly, of some of those who were not so great.

He thus emphasizes the importance of each teacher—as Dr. Glading begins by actually taking the eight-letter word *TEACHERS* and creatively and effectively building an eight-chapter analysis in this book around each of the letters—as an acronym, making the book absolutely "acronymic."

As one example, let's take the first letter in TEACHERS, the letter *T*, which becomes the very heart of instruction—*techniques* of teaching, the very essence and basics of the profession. Glading then lays out the critical importance of what *teaching techniques* entail, such as instruction and exploration. This leads teachers and classrooms to being "student centered," involving things like group work and discussions. And the first chapter on the *T* in TEACHERS ends with a discussion of technology, which has become critical to learning and knowledge in the modern high-tech world—and a real resource for teachers.

And teachers, he stresses, are critical to our lives and memories of years in school.

Glading, thus, reminds us in this book to remember the following: "We all remember those teachers who had a keen wit and sense of humor. . . . We recall those classes as being a 'breath of fresh air' during a physically and mentally draining and stifling day. Students need to be motivated to learn, and master teachers weave humor into the fabric of their instruction."

And the "S" at the end of TEACHERS conveys the personal *style* of the teachers—and of their classes and lessons. Teaching is one of the world's great genuine professional practices—meaningful relations in the lives of our children. For Glading argues, convincingly, in this book that teaching is a "performing art," like acting, musical instrument performance, dancing, or singing. Hence, it's essential that a teacher is self-confident, and comfortable "in his or her own skin." No job is more public, interactive, and important than teaching. Style matters to students—and to teachers as working colleagues!

VIEWS OF TEACHING FROM FOUR PROFESSIONAL PERSPECTIVES

After the eight parts and framework applications based on the word and eight letters in TEACHERS are explained and applied, this fascinating book provides four perspectives on education in schools from key actors on the scene, including: (1) a principal's, (2) a teacher's, (3) a parent's, and then from (4) a therapist's viewpoint. The book thus ends on a meaningful, sensitive, *personal* level, urging teachers to act as therapists to their students and their families. As one person explains: "In *The Qualities of a Master Teacher Today*, Dr. Glading captures the key attributes of highly effective educators. As a high school principal and assistant principal for twenty-four years, I had the pleasure of working with hundreds of teachers. I believe this book succinctly outlines the key content knowledge, pedagogical skills, habits of mind, and dispositions possessed by successful teachers." In Hillary Clinton's best seller *It Takes a Village*, the message is loud and clear: all adults involved in a child's life are expected to provide support and guidance—and help.

THE FOUR PERSPECTIVES ON TEACHING AND TEACHERS

Perspective 1—The Principal

In chapter 9, Glading provides the data from an interview with a principal about teaching and education. This principal thinks that teaching is easy, perhaps too easy. As the interviewed principal explains, "There is nothing particularly difficult about teaching. Everyone has the capacity to teach something. For a classroom teacher, it would be easy to make copies of a series of worksheets, hand the worksheets out to students, collect the worksheets, place grades on the worksheets, hand the worksheets back to students, and use the grades to calculate an average for end-of-quarter, end-of-semester, and end-of-year grades."

But as the principal further explains, teaching can also be the "most difficult job" in the world, if teachers do it correctly, with full reflection—and if they totally immerse themselves in their work—and do it best!

Perspective 2—The Teacher

This perspective is critical, as teachers teach and work directly with the children in their classes on a daily school basis. The teacher in chapter 10 asks these questions concerning her role and effectiveness: *"How can I improve? Am I doing enough? How can I motivate and engage my students while still offering rigorous lessons that challenge them? Are they learning?"* And the teacher's viewpoint on her teaching and students' learning is: "How does a master teacher, then, ensure that students learn? You must put them as the focal point. It seems obvious, but it's actually something that many teachers struggle with. Many teachers still believe they teach their content."

Perspective 3: The Parent

Many parents are not themselves "trained educators," and this parent admits this right away in chapter 11, as follows: "I am not a professional educator, nor have I been trained in the ways of school administration, so I offer only anecdotal information that highlights some of the successful experiences my children have had over the past ten years."

The parent tells a story of her child's experience with grammar and writing in an English class, which were important to both the parent and the child: "Mr. Thurman taught three courses: AP Language and Composition, satire, and a ninth-grade composition course. He possessed a very strong personality and was very direct with all the students. He never sugarcoated his feedback and let them know when their work was subpar and in need of vast improvement."

This anecdote underlines the reality that "good teachers" don't have to be "easy teachers." Rather, from this perspective, good teachers teach skills, and her kids learned from them. And a high school teacher in an advanced history course was tough and strong and demanding, which this parent liked, as reported: "He was an incredibly engaging lecturer whose knowledge of U.S. and world history was impressive. He could authoritatively speak on numerous topics and provide extensive answers to seemingly any question, including references to other regions of the world or other important issues of the era in question."

Perspective 4—The Therapist

And the fourth and final perspective is that of the therapist, where schools and teachers become "therapists" to the children who need them, sometimes desperately. Take this child who was being bullied by the child's peers in school and was living in an unstable situation at home as an example from chapter 12: "Ultimately, the bullying subsided and a relationship was formed between the teacher and my patient's parent that allowed this parent to get involved in the school by becoming a class parent (yes, they still do exist!). This master teacher saw that this family system was in a difficult way and opened up the classroom to enable positive change. Teachers don't only teach to the children; often it is the extended family where many life lessons are learned."

IN CONCLUSION

Thus, we are so glad for Dr. Randall Glading—and for us as readers of this book! He has given the world of educators and families real guidance about their TEACHERS, letter by letter—and the perspectives of a real parent, teacher, principal, and therapist about their views of education and what these folks have to say about teaching.

One of my professors in the University of Chicago doctoral program, Daniel C. Lortie, would truly enjoy this book were he still active today. His great and famous book, *Schoolteacher: A Sociological Study*, has been published twice (1975 and 2002) and truly explains the loneliness of working behind the "classroom door" with little support from colleagues and administrators. While most "professionals" collaborate and work closely, teachers work mostly alone. Teachers are thus deemed "semiprofessional," as they, too, often work alone.

For as chapter 9 explains so well, "In order to meet the needs of every student, an effective teacher possesses the ability to form meaningful relationships. Effective teachers create meaningful relationships through genuine, personal, and authentic interactions with students, parents, and colleagues. A chain is only as strong as its weakest link, and a school community is only as strong as its weakest relationship."

Bruce S. Cooper, PhD, is professor emeritus at Fordham University, Graduate School of Education; he also has taught at the University of London Institute of Education, Dartmouth College, and University of Pennsylvania. He has written some forty-four books, and two hundred articles, including two books on homeschooling and two editions of the Handbook of Education Politics and Policy *with Lance Fusarelli and James Cibulka. He is "retired" in New York City but still writing (see above).*

PREFACE

The profession of teaching has experienced radical change over the past several years. The movement away from traditional teaching styles has opened up the classroom to exciting and innovative learning experiences. Every day students participate in activities that elicit higher-order thinking skills and inquiry. These creative teaching techniques place the child in the center of learning. The entire school community needs to understand these current pedagogical practices.

The role of the teacher has also evolved over time. Teachers are looked upon today to do so much more, to be responsible for the academic, social, and emotional growth of the child. It is important that all members of an academic community, administrators, teachers, parents, and students understand the qualities that embody a master teacher today. In addition, aspiring individuals in teacher preparation programs need to understand what lies ahead and the evolution of pedagogy.

Effective teaching is the foundation of every academic community. The establishment of a positive culture for learning is the responsibility of each and every teacher. It is also critically important that parents, grandparents, and family understand what it means to be an effective teacher. After all, they are the first teachers in the life of a child.

Upon completion of this text, the goal is for all members of the academic community to understand the qualities of a master teacher. School administrators will be able to look at their teachers through several different lenses and identify certain qualities of teachers that at times are not emphasized in the teacher evaluation process. Teachers will be encouraged to reflect upon their own practices to meet the needs of every student and provide students with learning opportunities to reach their full potential. Parents will be able to understand what effective teaching involves and what should be occurring in the classroom every day and apply those same concepts to their day-to-day teaching of their child. Enjoy!

ACKNOWLEDGMENTS

This publication would not have been possible without the help and support of several individuals.

First and foremost, I need to thank my family for their ongoing support and motivation. My wife, Laura, and my son, Thomas, served as my GPS throughout this journey.

A special thanks to Jessica Gleason, a new mother and English teacher, who took time out of her hectic life to edit my text.

Lastly, I need to thank four individuals who have provided the readers with their personal and professional perspective of the concepts set forth in this text.

Dr. Charles Britton, who provided a perspective as a former high school principal.

Alison Rodilosso, who presented her perspective through the lens of a parent of four children.

Jessica Gleason, who provided her perspective as a high school English teacher.

Amy Bernstein, who provided input through the lens of a licensed therapist.

INTRODUCTION
Memories

When we look back at our years of formal education, we have both fond and troubling memories. We remember the exciting life that we were exposed to in elementary school, along with the unknown day-to-day challenges that we would face. Upon completion of those introductory years to public or private education, we were thrust into the turmoil of adolescence and expected to be successful climbing through a variety of academic, social, and emotional experiences.

As we reflect on these experiences, we remember those individuals who have touched our lives in a special way. What was it about Mrs. Jones, a fourth-grade teacher at West End Elementary School, who has impacted the lives of so many children? Or Tony Seaman, teacher and lacrosse coach, who conducted those long conversations about being a teenager and making good decisions? Or Dr. Bruce Cooper, a renowned professor and mentor in the doctoral program at Fordham University, who would never directly answer a question and would prod all of the members of our cohort to look at things differently?

Every day in our schools, students continue to have these experiences. In every school, wonderful educators have an impact on individuals for life. The goal of this book is to highlight the qualities that these individuals possess and to inform parents, teachers, administrators, and students of the qualities of a master teacher: the individual who has made a difference in the lives of many. Due to their influence on their students, these teachers have had an impact on generations of people, many of whom they will never meet.

There is no specific course of study or curriculum that creates a master teacher. There are no specific experiences, either, that will ensure that a beginning teacher becomes a master teacher. This text will look at the qualities of a master teacher through several different perspectives that after reading you will be able to sit back, reflect and say yes, that is what made that fifth-grade science teacher special. In addition, this book is designed to make sense to anyone who reads it. You do not have to be a school administrator or educator to grasp the overarching concepts of what makes a master teacher today!

EFFECTIVE USE OF THIS BOOK FOR EDUCATORS

This book will provide several references including renowned texts and peer-reviewed articles. However, with the use of technology and our ability to search for topics within educational research databases, it is recommended that as you read this book, you open up either ERIC or Educational Research Complete from your school or university library.

For example, if you are interested in finding scholarly journals under the topic of differentiation of instruction or individualized instruction, you simply search in these databases under peer-reviewed articles. This will ensure that the articles that you read are grounded in educational research.

In a recent search, there were 4,103 journals, articles, or research studies in the ERIC database and 1,380 entries in the Educational Research Complete database under the topic of differentiation or individualized instruction. Utilizing this strategy will open up the world of research, thus providing you with varying opinions, strategies, and examples on the implementation of this effective instructional technique.

FOR ALL OTHER MEMBERS OF THE SCHOOL COMMUNITY

This book is intended to address a wide audience. In Hillary Clinton's best seller *It Takes a Village* (Clinton, 1996), she highlights the important role that all adults play in raising a child. Parents, grandparents, family, and friends are usually the child's first teachers.

Therefore, it is important that individuals not involved in education have an opportunity to further their understanding of the contents of this text through a portal for which they have access and convenience. You can access articles and entries that are not research based, usually articles from journals or entries by teachers in the field who are willing to share their expertise and experiences. This can be done by simply entering the keyword in your search browser. Recently I conducted a search on the topic of differentiation in teaching and there were twenty-five million resources.

In addition, at the end of the text are four final chapters, each titled "Perspectives." These chapters are written by four individuals: a principal, teacher, parent, and therapist. Each was given the table of contents of the book and was asked to reflect upon the concepts—without seeing the text—from their perspective. This will provide the reader with an unbiased account of the overarching concepts of what it takes to be a master teacher today. It is evident through the varying writing styles that these four chapters have not been edited or altered in any way.

PUBLIC EDUCATION: WHERE ARE WE TODAY?

In order to understand where we are today regarding education, you will be provided with a brief overview of several initiatives that have been presented to public education over the years. The infamous *A Nation at Risk* report in 1983 ignited a flurry of educational reform initiatives over the past thirty years.

Following this historical educational report, our country was immersed in legislation from President Bush's administration, specifically No Child Left Behind in 2001. It impacted what students were taught, when students were to be assessed using standardized tests, and how teachers were prepared. This act also required schools to meet certain standards. If schools failed to meet their goals, parents in those schools were given options for their child to attend a higher-performing school and in some cases schools were taken over by the state and restructured.

Recently, under President Obama's administration, school districts are grappling with the mandates set forth in the Race to the Top initiative as they are forced to revise and implement new policies and procedures, which directly affects the day-to-day instruction in every classroom. Effective instruction has been one of the foci of the Race to the Top federal program, as it clearly should be. The effectiveness of every lesson in every classroom is the most important tenet of the educational philosophy of any academic community.

Therefore, the emphasis has been shifted to the revision of teacher evaluation systems with an emphasis, for the first time in the history of teaching, on implementing a quantitative system of professional review where teachers will receive a quantitative evaluation (numerical grade) for their overall job performance. Individual states were *required* to revise their teacher evaluations systems under this law to ensure that struggling teachers were identified, monitored, and supported with professional development and in some cases, terminated.

The new evaluation systems for teachers include several aspects of teaching that in many cases may have been overlooked in the past. The works of Charlotte Danielson, William Glasser, and Kim Marshall, along with many other leaders in the field of education, have highlighted these essential qualities of a master teacher in their writings and evaluation frameworks (Danielson, 2014; Glasser, 1999; Marshall, 2013).

The current evaluation system being implemented looks at the art of teaching through a new lens. The language has changed and the focus is placing the student in the center of the learning process. This is a departure from traditional teaching.

Many aspects of effective teaching will be presented in this book. Using a simple acronym, you will not only be able to identify each aspect of effective teaching, but it will be easy to recall and remember the ideas that the letter represents. This book will highlight certain attributes that a teacher and administrator must possess to be successful in education today. These qualities have been embedded into the current evaluation systems being implemented across the country.

Effective teaching today involves so much more!

WHAT IT TAKES TO BE A MASTER TEACHER TODAY

The main portion of the text will include eight chapters: each chapter titled with a letter in the acronym TEACHERS. The letters represent the following traits that a master teacher possesses. The author's explanation of each trait will ring true for many of us as we reflect back to that teacher who made a profound difference in our lives.

T—Technique: Instructional Strategies
E—Empathy: Step into the Student's Shoes
A—Assessment: Monitoring Student Understanding and Progress
C—Content: Your Academic Discipline
H—Humor: Making Minds Smile
E—Energy: Leading a Positive Culture for Learning
R—Relationships: Creating That Special Bond
S—Style: A Unique, Personal Approach

The art of teaching has evolved. By remembering the acronym and what each letter represents, this work will allow us to remember the most important qualities of a master teacher today!

Example 1

A ninth-grade English teacher has a student in her class who has never been successful in the ELA (English language arts) content area. He is extremely disorganized, misses several homework assignments, and minimally passes his assessments. He is an English language learner from the Dominican Republic and has been in the country for four years. The teacher finds out, however, that this student is an excellent football player.

In order to understand her students better, she creates a list of the activities that her students participate in after school and dedicates an entire wall in her classroom to highlight their interests and talents and vows to attend one of their competitions. Through her conversations with her students, she discovers four other students in the class who play football. She attends the football game and asks permission to be on the sidelines to take some pictures with her iPhone.

She posts the pictures of the students on the wall in her class, right next to this reluctant student's desk. The student is currently proud to walk into his English class and has begun to take ownership of his work. He has built a special bond with the teacher. William Glasser, the author of *The Quality School*, would describe this teacher's action as entering the quality world of that student. The teacher has created and will continue to nurture this special bond (Glasser, 1999).

Example 2

In addition to providing an appropriate educational program to meet the needs of every child, schools are also responsible for the emotional and social growth of their students. Social workers and school psychologists work tirelessly to ensure that every child is supported during their years of schooling. A child's teachers play an integral role in supporting their students through challenging times.

In one case, a parent questions the way a teacher or school official is handling a delicate, sensitive situation regarding his child. That parent would immediately reflect upon the letter *E*, which represents empathy, remembering how important it is for educators to empathize with individuals and care about them. The parent would be able to discuss the situation through the lens of a caring parent and ask that the teacher look at the situation differently in a developmental and caring manner. These are conversations that teachers have every day with students and families and is a common thread woven into the fabric of a master teacher and a supportive school culture.

Example 3

The final example would involve instruction. A student is struggling in mathematics class, and it is obvious that the student is not an auditory learner and has poor note-taking skills. The class is taught in a traditional lecture format where the students are passive learners. The teacher is obviously comfortable with this style of teaching; however, effective instructional strategies involve a range of educational experiences to provide students with a productive learning environment.

This teacher would be able to reflect upon the technique portion of the text that provides information regarding different effective teaching strategies that teachers can employ to meet the needs of all students with varying learning styles. The incorporation of effective scaffolding

T:
TECHNIQUE
Instructional Strategies

The term *technique* is defined as "the method of procedure in rendering an artistic work or carrying out a scientific or mechanical operation" (*Webster's*, 1983, pg. 1872). The profession of teaching is no different than other professions in that an individual's technique is used to perform certain tasks to be successful. Whether you are a professional golfer, surgeon, attorney, or hedge fund manager, one needs to hone various techniques to attain excellence.

In regard to teaching, the term *technique* encompasses a plethora of concepts, ranging from specific instructional practices used to offer the students an exciting and engaging learning experience to implementing specific strategies to meet the individual needs of the learner (Meyers, Molefe, & Brandt, 2015). The concept of "one size fits all" when it comes to learning activities in today's classroom no longer exists. For years, however, the traditional lecture format was acceptable as noted by Albert Einstein, one of the greatest thinkers in modern history:

> It is in fact nothing short of a miracle that the modern methods of instruction have not yet entirely strangled the holy curiosity of inquiry: for this delicate little plant, aside from stimulation, stands mainly in need of freedom, without this it goes to wrack and ruin without fail. (Quoted in Glading, 2008, p. 48)

The effective teacher today has been transformed from basically a provider of information to a facilitator of effective pedagogy. Today's teachers are expected to lead their students along the continuum of knowledge and inquiry, providing an exciting learning environment by placing students in the center of the learning process and allowing them to take ownership of their learning.

Oftentimes we forget the definition of the term *educate*. The term comes from Latin roots

- *educare*, which means to bring up, rear, or train a child;
- *ducere*, to lead, draw, bring; and
- *educe* (modern English term), which comes from the same two Latin roots. The formal definition of *educe* is to bring or draw out, to elicit, to evolve, to deduce, to infer from data.

Our modern-day definition of the term *educate* has been defined by the traditional educational practices that have been in place for years. If we refer back to the previous quote by Albert Einstein, it is quite interesting that one of the most brilliant individuals of the twentieth century understood the shortcomings of our educational system so long ago.

The traditional instructional strategy he is referring to is lecture, where the teacher provides information to students and they are engaged as "passive learners." This instructional format was the norm in our public schools for years, replicating the "factory" model of learning developed during the Industrial Revolution. The Latin roots of the word *educate* include so much more, which will be supported by the instructional strategies set forth in this text.

Potential teachers take methodology courses to learn effective strategies to educate their students. These undergraduate programs, however, are oftentimes being taught by professors who use traditional methods of teaching, reinforcing the role of the learner as passive and receptive. At some time in our educational experience we have seen a glimpse of effective teaching: activities that placed the learner in the center of learning, requiring each and every one of us in the cohort to *think*. This should not be a novel concept in our schools.

Graduate programs offer potential teachers and teachers who are currently working with a wide range of experiences to introduce current initiatives and develop some level of proficiency and knowledge regarding the art of teaching either prior to their entrance into the workforce or while they are novice teachers. The use of student teaching experiences and fieldwork observations during coursework provides prospective teachers with a taste of things to come.

Individuals entering the field, however, are sometimes ill informed and unaware that the instructional techniques and teaching strategies have experienced a catharsis since their own school years. Instruction is quite different from the traditional lecture format that many of us experienced in our formal schooling.

While the bureaucracy we call school over the years has been quite resistant to change, instructional techniques continue to evolve. Our school buildings continue to represent the factory model established in the early 1900s due to the influence of the Industrial Revolution; however, inside each learning unit—the classroom—effective teachers are implementing innovative instructional techniques and learning is fun, exciting, and engaging.

INSTRUCTION

All the intricacies of effective instruction cannot be effectively discussed in one short chapter. What you will be offered, however, is an overview of effective strategies that are used by master teachers. This overview, coupled with all the other dimensions of effective teaching noted in this text, will provide all educators and parents with a solid understanding of the activities and strategies that we expect teachers to implement on a daily basis.

Instruction is just one aspect of pedagogy that is supported by all of the salient portions of this text. When we visualize what instruction looks like, many of us identify lecture as a common practice. When we enter a classroom, we open our notebooks and prepare to become passive learners. We were well trained.

When we look at Bloom's taxonomy, which was developed during the 1950s, it becomes quite evident that there were several shortcomings regarding the nature of instruction in our schools. It is quite disappointing that we still emphasize standardized testing and the memorization of facts as the bar being set in our schools. Effective teachers view the need to recall specific facts as a by-product of what goes on in their classroom, a minimal accomplishment of each student during their school year.

Effective teachers teach way "beyond the test." Bloom notes that the memorization of facts and one's ability to recall that information is the lowest form of intellectual engagement, which he calls knowledge.

The 1956 version of Bloom's taxonomy is an accurate representation of the teaching practices of that era. The attainment of knowledge and one's ability to recall that information was a basic tenet of day-to-day teaching. The use of lecture and passive note taking was commonplace in every classroom (Bloom, 1956).

The revised version of Bloom's taxonomy inverts the triangle and places a greater emphasis on higher-order thinking skills. This clearly defines the current focus of effective instruction today. Whereas it is important to understand facts and recall information, the emphasis must be placed on creative thinking, evaluating, analyzing, and applying. An emphasis on these higher-order thinking skills will automatically provide each and every student with an understanding of the concepts and the ability to recall information (Anderson, 2001).

EXPLORATION

It would be fascinating to look at the world through the lens of a newborn and follow his constant exploration of the world around him. Many

Bloom's taxonomy.

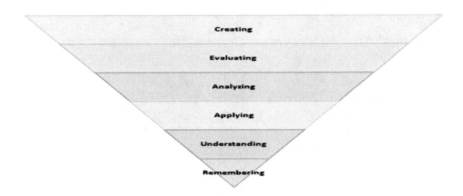

Bloom's taxonomy revised.

child development theories emphasize the rapid growth of cognitive development through children's constant observation and interpretation of their environment. Through trial and error, children learn that certain objects around them are soft, hard, hot, and cold, just to mention a few physical characteristics of our environment.

However, with the increasing emphasis on data collection and quantitative assessment techniques, teachers tend to circle the wagons and teach to the test. With the new teacher evaluation procedures being put in place across our country, the emphasis on test performance has never been greater. This is clearly a distraction from innovative teaching strategies.

Students of all ages need to be involved in instructional environments that foster exploration. Through exploration, the level of inquiry will flourish and the child will become an independent learner. This will elicit the learner to ask why, not what. Effective teaching releases the student into the world of exploration.

This occurs at any grade level or content area. When students are permitted to explore, the students take ownership of their learning and the work becomes personal, as something that they found that is relevant to what they are learning. It is exciting and engaging and allows the students to make connections between what they are learning and the world in which they live.

Master teachers are constantly placing the student in the center of the learning process and learning activities that require students to explore, investigate, and engage in higher-order thinking skills through their inquiry of the world around them. These activities need to be developed in all academic disciplines, providing children with an exciting and interactive learning environment.

STUDENT-CENTERED LEARNING

Placing the student in the center of learning is a method used to enhance, displace, and redirect the ownership for learning on each individual student. A master teacher who engages his or her students and places them in the center of the learning process provides the framework for academic rigor and relevant learning.

Student-centered learning can have many different faces. Master teachers weave this technique into classroom activities, student-centered projects, assessment strategies, cooperative learning activities, and independent research projects. This technique, however, will take years to hone to perfection, and will involve trial and error and the teacher taking some risks. Today's administrators, however, do not view these risks as a weakness; they are viewed as a strength and an essential part of the arsenal of a maverick, or master, teacher.

Hands-on learning activities are an essential instructional technique and a critical aspect of student-centered learning that should be incorporated in all disciplines. The use of manipulatives supports kinesthetic learners and provides a concrete visual and physical example of a concept, which at times can be abstract and difficult for all students to understand. This strategy also supports differentiated instruction to meet the needs of a diverse learning community.

This is the beauty of teaching today. Traditional instruction tended to be only goal oriented and the final number in an assessment was the bottom line. Whereas assessment is still a critical part of education today, teachers are given many options to attain this success and student-centered learning is one of those tools. It makes learning fun, engaging, and relevant to our students.

The shift to student-centered learning is one of the basic tenets of the work of Charlotte Danielson. In order for a teacher to be exemplary, the student needs to be placed in the center of the learning process and be actively engaged. The practice of teacher-centered instruction providing information to passive learners is something of the past. This shift, however, contradicts how many individuals entering the teaching profession were taught and is challenging to young teachers who were exposed to the traditional model of learning.

The concept of having students take responsibility for their learning is one of the results of student-centered learning. The active engagement of the student requires that the students take ownership for their learning. This concept is a breath of fresh air for our students, allowing them to become active and engaged learners, as opposed to passive learners who are asked to memorize information that they may never use again in their lifetime.

Master teachers who have established an effective culture for learning in their classroom understand and implement this concept on a daily basis. One result of this evolution in teaching is that classrooms have become louder, with student discourse and inquiry providing the foundation for authentic and genuine learning.

This evolution in teaching is quite obvious and evident once you enter the classroom as an observer. Over the past twenty-five years, schools have placed students in both positive and toxic classroom cultures. Upon entering a classroom of a master teacher who places the child at the center of learning, administrators enjoy sitting back and looking at the involvement and engagement of the students in their learning. The students enter the classroom with a sense of excitement and anticipation, are immersed in their learning during the lesson, and at the end of the lesson they are intellectually satisfied and proud of their accomplishments.

DISCUSSION

The use of discussion has been a common instructional practice in many classrooms. Certain disciplines tend to incorporate more discussion than others so there is no specific template for when discussion should be used. However, certain guidelines need to be followed if a teacher is looking to provide the students with an effective and engaging experience.

Effective classroom cultures provide an opportunity for students to speak freely and take risks. Students should feel acknowledged in their participation in discussion activities and their participation needs to be validated and supported. This will allow the students to look for a deeper meaning and be led down the path of higher-order thinking.

This concept is true in all work environments and learning institutions. We feel validated when we are allowed to participate freely in discussions at work or on the job. The building of human capital (positive buy-in by individuals and support within a school or organization) creates a positive organizational culture and promotes individual success and ongoing accomplishments. Students' input needs to be embraced and acknowledged in the classroom, and one of the venues to do so is through open discussion.

Paulo Freire, the famous educational innovator who was constantly looking to support the oppressed in public education, identified one aspect of effective discussion. He penned that educators need to participate in what he called *apprehending*. This was defined as taking in and making meaning of claims by individuals participating in a discussion. As an effective facilitator of learning, master teachers interpret, process, inquire, and understand the concepts set forth by their students in discussion activities (Freire, 1997).

The effective use of discussion activities is also addressed in a later section about the Socratic method, where the teacher leads the students using constant questioning in the search for the answer, concept, or truth.

GROUP WORK

The incorporation of cooperative learning activities in day-to-day instruction has become commonplace. When utilizing this instructional strategy, however, extensive planning is a requirement. Once the locus of control that is prevalent in direct teacher-student instruction is no longer present, the organization of materials and individuals becomes paramount. There have been many successful cooperative learning activities along with those that have failed terribly.

The basic tenets of cooperative learning activities are structure, planning, establishing clear goals, providing clear and succinct directions, and understanding the culture for learning that the class possesses. This is greatly dependent upon the individual personalities of the class and the subtle, yet powerful, student world that you are orchestrating.

The organization of cooperative learning groups has been the subject of extensive educational studies. As adults, we have all been involved in committees that have been given a charge that is expected to be resolved. Many times we fall short, due to strong personalities and varying opinions. All we need to do is look at the current state of our democratic government to understand the dynamics of cooperative decision making and learning.

One of the most important aspects of assigning cooperative learning groups is balance. There are several characteristics of these groups that require balance. These characteristics include student personalities, academic ability, individual skills, vocation, and personal experiences. Master teachers organize their cooperative learning activities so that all the participants experience success, with each of the individuals contributing to the charges presented.

Novice teachers need to understand that they will experience both success and certain hurdles as they introduce cooperative learning activities. The possibility of challenges and even failure, however, should never discourage teachers from taking risks to enhance their educational offerings. Students benefit greatly from cooperative learning activities, and the benefits greatly outweigh the possibility of a learning activity that falls short of the teacher's expectations. Once again, fully understanding the dynamics of cooperative learning will provide a foundation for success.

HIGHER-ORDER THINKING SKILLS

When young children present us with profound and intriguing statements, we immediately acknowledge that they are gifted. Young children lack certain filters that older children possess and they are constantly making inquiries about the world in which they live. The old expression "from the mouths of babes" continues to ring loud and true.

There are many educators who believe that the reason that older children may not embrace higher-order thinking skills is due to the fact that they have been immersed in an education system that stifles creative thinking and inquiry. This has been the topic of several studies and there is some truth to this claim. Recent trends in elementary education support the notion that higher-order thinking skills and inquiry need to be introduced on a daily basis.

However, it is unfortunate that some teachers still feel the need to teach to the test, thus limiting students' exposure to authentic learning experiences. Traditional public education has stifled one's need to think, explore, and inquire for decades. Schools have groomed passive learners, children who sit and wait to record the information disseminated to them by an expert in the discipline. At the end of the activity or unit, a number measures success.

Master teachers find a way to elicit higher-order thinking skills in all children, no matter their age or ability. The learning activities in the classroom are alive, exciting, engaging, productive, and fun. Over the course of our formal years of schooling, we all remember these special individuals.

Once again, however, this is not an easy skill to master. The incorporation of individual student personalities, eliciting of creative information from students who may have been conditioned to be passive learners, and the developmental level of the student place hurdles in the path to individual accomplishments. The master teacher, however, finds a way to clear these obstacles and walk with each and every child along their personal continuum of success.

PROJECT-BASED LEARNING

This instructional technique allows the child to take control of his learning. When a student develops a project that results in a final product that he can call his own, the learning experience is genuine. Providing the student with the academic freedom to create his or her own project is a powerful learning activity.

One example of project-based learning involves the most advanced students in a traditional high school, the science research students. These students have the freedom to create research-based projects on a topic they are passionate about, work with researchers in the field, and compete at national and international competitions. The research projects are extremely impressive and the learning experience is extremely rewarding.

Why is this extensive project-based learning model limited to this small group of advanced students while all the mainstream students are exposed to traditional instructional strategies? Project-based learning should be incorporated into the instruction of every classroom.

Students today have an incredible advantage through the evolution of the Internet. Project-based learning does, however, involve extensive planning and preparation. As easily as the Internet provides one with an unlimited amount of information, teaching children proper research strategies has become an integral part of all curriculum guides and their corresponding curriculum maps. All teachers, as early as elementary school, are expected to incorporate technology and research into their instruction.

Project-based learning has many different faces, but actually, they are all the same. The project placed in front of a second grader may appear to be quite different from a multiyear extensive research project at the secondary level. But actually, the only difference is the developmental level of the children and the goals set forth by a master teacher.

This form of independent learning is utilized across all curriculums and varies in depth and breadth. For example, a humanities project may involve looking at the family structure across several cultures and looking at their differences and similarities, whereas a science research project may involve years of intense, narrow research on the effect of a specific drug on a specific group of children. Both of these projects support a vital vocation for all students and give them the opportunity to find their way through a plethora of information and develop a meaningful and authentic product.

EXPERIENTIAL LEARNING

Experiential learning is the process of learning through our experiences, many of which may be coordinated with the school community or community at large. Master teachers weave experiential learning into their curriculum to enhance their course offerings and provide students with connections to the real world.

As part of the curriculum, a social studies teacher may have his students engage in Habitat for Humanity where students will volunteer to build homes for individuals who are less fortunate or have been impacted by a natural disaster. Participation in Habitat for Humanity provides all participants with an experience that will contribute to their personal growth, a deeper understanding of socioeconomic differences, and an exposure to various cultures. The personal growth and individual learning that occurs on these trips will be remembered for a lifetime.

The opportunities for experiential learning are limitless. How often does an earth science teacher take her class on field trips where they can actually look at parts of the earth or natural phenomena, or the art history teacher take her class to the Metropolitan Museum of Art, or the world history teacher take her students away for a weekend to the Holocaust Museum in Washington, D.C.?

Organized classroom trips are a rather large undertaking, and there needs to be extensive organization and planning. But how often do we encourage students to engage in experiential learning on their own and with their family and then share their experiences with the class? These opportunities provide the opportunity for students to bring their experiences into the classroom and make teaching and learning personal. Novice teachers must realize this is a powerful teaching strategy. This is another way to place the student in the center of learning to enhance and expand the classroom experience to real-world application.

ACADEMIC RIGOR

Academic rigor has been in the forefront of public education for decades. We can look back at the influence of Sputnik, *A Nation at Risk*, No Child Left Behind, and most recently Race to the Top. The rigor of the day-to-day instruction was the focus of these national initiatives.

Teachers are expected, as they should be, to challenge their students in their day-to-day instruction. Parents expect that their children will be encouraged to reach their academic potential and be prepared for postsecondary studies. The first twelve years in public education lay the foundation for educational opportunities beyond high school, and prepare the individual to become a productive member of society.

Master teachers strike the delicate balance between rigor and reality. Students need to be challenged but also need to be successful. Teachers who challenge students beyond their developmental level and allow them to fail are actually providing a positive experience that will motivate the individual to move forward only if it is framed in a certain way. Optional advanced work is important to allow students to reach their potential, but the results cannot be quantitative and have an impact on their overall grade and academic performance.

This is what great teachers do: place challenges in front of students, have them take risks, and reward them for their efforts. They do not punish them for their shortcomings.

The importance of academic rigor is quite obvious; however, in a recent documentary titled *The Race to Nowhere*, the policies and practices of schools and universities were challenged. This documentary was produced following the tragic loss of a high school student. This model student, after receiving a poor grade on an examination, committed suicide.

The documentary was produced by a friend of the family and offers a powerful discourse regarding the pressures placed on our students today. Once again, when we talk about academic rigor, we need to consider balance and look at the child's overall school experience: each teacher viewing a typical day of a student through the student lens.

But there is a reality that is often avoided in teacher-parent-student and counselor-parent-student conversations in secondary school. Post-secondary education continues to focus on quantitative data. It is important that we look at the overall child, but the stark reality is that the main factors regarding college admission are the student's GPA, SAT, or ACT scores and class rank.

Colleges and universities do consider other factors including school participation in clubs, community service, and other special accomplishments. One can argue, however, that this information is comfortably in the backseat when it comes to college admissions. To support this charge, please log onto the class profile of any class at any university. The university will provide you with the class profile that usually indicates the middle 50 percent of the students it admits.

In closing, academic rigor is still a critical part in determining the future of all secondary students. They need to be challenged in order to compete at the next level. This may be the eight-hundred-pound gorilla in the room that we fail to acknowledge. The master teacher will provide the opportunity for each and every child to be challenged and to ultimately reach his or her potential.

RELEVANCE

If we look back at our educational experiences, we were expected to memorize an inordinate number of facts and then be exposed to a quantitative examination, usually multiple choice, true or false, or short answer, for an assessment. In the humanities, more qualitative assessments were used from time to time to support student writing. This still holds true today when we look at the College Board and the SAT and ACT examinations. These assessments are used as a filtering mechanism by postsecondary academic institutions.

So the law of the land is still steeped deep in quantitative, right-or-wrong answers. However, master teachers lead students to the next level of learning. Although test taking is a skill that is fostered by effective teachers, it is considered by master professionals to be the minimum. Teachers who make a difference in their students open up a world of knowledge that is relevant to their students. Connections are made daily to the world around them and higher-order thinking skills are elicited and nurtured.

We have all had teachers in the past who have done this, but unfortunately they were few and far between. Public education over the past thirty years has immersed students into countless hours of lecture and memorization.

Learning today is vibrant and alive, and students are exposed to instruction that allows them to look at the world differently. Instead of asking, "What," students now are encouraged to ask, "Why?"

Master teachers in all content areas are determined to make their instruction relevant to their students and make connections to the world around them. There are certain content areas, however, where it is difficult to make the information being taught relevant to the day-to-day experiences of a student. Higher-level mathematics, for example, leads the student down a path of advanced abstract concepts that lack relevance. The master teacher, however, finds a way for these students to become excited about their efforts and achieve academic success.

It is critically important for master teachers to provide this connection and make the work relevant to the specific age group they are teaching. For example, word problems in mathematics are an area where there can be an application to a real-life situation. This connection is critical, especially for struggling students who fail to comprehend the abstract concepts in the mathematics curriculum. It is imperative to make learning fun, engaging, and meaningful to each and every student.

Willard Daggett redefined Bloom's taxonomy and created this "Rigor/Relevance Framework" model of learning.

The concepts in Bloom's revised taxonomy (remembering, understanding, applying, analyzing, evaluating, creating) are incorporated in the rigor scale presented by Daggett. An added dimension, relevance, describes the application of this knowledge to real-life situations.

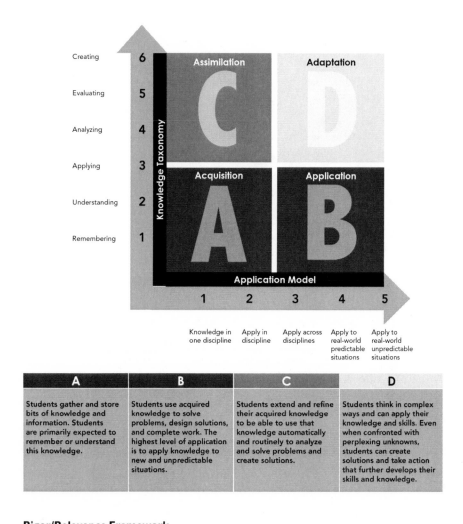

Rigor/Relevance Framework.

School districts across the country participate in professional development activities that incorporate the Rigor/Relevance Framework.
School districts adopt this program to move their districts forward and
enhance student learning, making it real and applicable to the day-to-
day experiences of their students (International Center for Leadership
in Education, 2016).

SOCRATIC METHOD

Obviously, the Socratic method has been around for a while, dating
back to the practices of Socrates in ancient Greece. All effective teachers, in all disciplines, weave the Socratic method of questioning and
eliciting information into their day-to-day instruction. All teachers
should be encouraged, no matter how experienced, to access information either in electronic or written form and fully understand and implement the Socratic method of teaching, since it is one of the most
powerful teaching tools that has been used for years by master teachers.

The Socratic method provides instruction that moves the students to
the pinnacle of the pyramid of learning as described in Bloom's taxonomy, and moves students into the most advanced quadrant of the Rigor/
Relevance paradigm. This instruction requires students to become engaged and respond to a never-ending stream of questions eliciting higher-order thinking skills.

The Socratic method, however, is a practice that takes years to master. The ability to drive classroom conversation utilizing an ongoing
stream of questions is developed over years of teaching and extensive
planning. It is also an art form, orchestrating the conversation of a
classroom of students to achieve a final outcome leading the individual
student into a world of higher-order thinking and inquiry.

This advanced questioning strategy places the student in the center
of learning. The teacher redirects questions to students and encourages
student-to-student discourse. The arrow of recitation moves from
teacher to student to student to student. Classrooms become alive and
the teacher assumes the role of facilitator, never giving out any information, just eliciting higher-order thinking and inquiry from the students.
It is a true art form that takes years to master but fosters an extremely
effective culture for learning.

SCAFFOLDING

Scaffolding is an instructional term that is used in all academic disciplines. It is not an advanced concept, but it involves chunking instruction into steps, or different levels of a scaffold, to reach a final goal. Once the students attain a certain level of understanding, the teacher can gradually release the students into student-centered learning activities. This instructional strategy is used daily in the classroom.

The concept of scaffolding in the classroom is very similar to learning how to walk. In the beginning, the parent will hold the child up with both hands and have him take "baby steps." This allows the child to experience the balance and muscular coordination required to walk independently. Then the child will advance to moving from object to object, falling frequently, but becoming more independent. Later, the child will be able to walk for a short duration and then fall. Finally, he will be able to walk on his own and it is time to go out and buy more safety gates.

Guiding our students and supporting them along the continuum of understanding is what great teachers do. The use of various instructional supports provides them with the tools to be successful and eventually work independently with confidence and success. The goal of placing students in the center of learning and having them take responsibility for their accomplishments is the goal of any effective lesson. We all remember the teachers who mastered this craft, and it was not an accident that we were involved in a productive learning environment.

DIFFERENTIATION

It is imperative that all teachers differentiate instruction on a daily basis to address the learning needs of every individual child in their class (Ikwumelu, Oyibe, & Oketa, 2015). The days of one size fits all is long gone and teachers need to model their instruction to ensure that each and every child in their class is successful. Would we go to a doctor who boasted that she was able to successfully treat 75 percent of her patients? I think not!

Novice teachers will be challenged by this expectation at the onset of their career. However, they have little time to incorporate this into their day-to-day instruction. It has become an expectation from the first day of class. New teachers with potential get it done and spend inordinate amounts of time working with administrators and seasoned faculty members to ensure that they are meeting the needs of every student.

Teachers are required to meet the needs of all types of students, for example, students with special learning needs, whether they have a learning disability or emotional handicap or are gifted. Teachers understand the legal expectation of meeting the needs of a child with an IEP or 504 Plan, which is carefully scripted in a document developed by a team of professionals at the building or district level.

There are also those students who are gifted and talented, with high-pressure parents who constantly ask, "How are you challenging my child?" But there is also the group in the middle, sometimes referred to as faces in the crowd, who are successful at their studies and very rarely raise a red flag.

There are many students who land in the middle, maintaining an 85–90 average and everyone appears satisfied, playing sports and representing the school in several after-school activities in the arts and athletics. The parents are happy and could not be prouder. The school and teachers also appear satisfied. In so many cases these students have so much more potential and are not pushed to reach their individual potential. This describes hundreds of students in every high school across the country today, living in a protective and insular adolescent society.

All students need to be pushed to their limits and reach their potential. The students in the middle are shortchanged every day in our schools, being offered limited differentiated activities to move them up the continuum of success and achievement. Master teachers do not settle for average work for students who have great potential; instead, they build positive relationships with them and constantly remind their students of their lofty, yet attainable, expectations.

The basic practices of differentiated instruction are quite simple; the challenging part is implementing the practices every day in class. First and foremost, students may require content presented at different levels. For example, in elementary reading, students will be offered leveled readers to ensure understanding and personal success. Success and rewards are the greatest motivators.

The teacher may also engage students in different learning activities to meet individual needs. Individual learning styles and personal strengths and weaknesses can be addressed by providing a variety of learning strategies.

The teacher may also need to change the learning environment where the student is working. Additional support and individualized instruction in a quiet setting or learning center set up in the room may provide the support that the child needs.

Differentiation is also used when the teacher is assessing the performance of the student. Alternate forms of assessment, such as portfolios, individual projects, guided test taking, scaffolding of evaluation tools, or participation in group presentations are a few ways in which the teacher can differentiate assessment. Alternative assignments can ensure student success and continuously motivate them to reach their potential.

TEACHABLE MOMENTS

Master teachers elicit higher-order thinking skills in every lesson. Beginning teachers, on the other hand, are oftentimes so concerned about their effective execution of an organized plan that critical thinking may be inhibited. Teachable moments, however, can surface in any lesson at any time. The master teacher will take a student-generated thought and mold it into the lesson and place the experience or thought of a student at the center of learning. This is a skill that master teachers hone over their years of teaching.

For the novice teacher, however, teachable moments may appear as a diversion into uncharted waters that at times seem treacherous and uncertain. All teachers need to infuse teachable moments into their day-to-day instruction. Teachers need to take risks to provide their students with authentic and genuine instruction.

When teachable moments occur during an evaluation, it is normal to be concerned about inserting the experience or thought of a student into the lesson. This, however, is the beauty of pedagogy, and as an instructor, one should be inspired and passionate about student input into a lesson. Any evaluator who understands master teaching should encourage the infusion of teachable moments into a lesson, even at the cost of not completing the planned tasks. The elicitation of higher-order thinking skills should be encouraged in any lesson.

Hopefully, you have all experienced a master teacher listening to your input as the genesis of a discussion or conversation in class. We remember how important, involved, and intelligent we felt at that moment, and the classroom became our world. Have you experienced walking out of class with your peers saying things like, "Wow, that was an awesome concept you brought up; the teacher loved it"? You couldn't wait to go home and tell your parents!

There are times, however, when a teacher might have ignored our comments and actually made critical comments regarding our input. In the twelve years of public schooling we are unfortunately exposed to poor teaching. We should all learn from those experiences.

STUDENT MANAGEMENT

Student management has an important place in the techniques chapter because it is a concern of all teachers, especially those starting out in the field. Throughout this text many characteristics of a master teacher will be discussed, and the development of these vocations will ensure seamless student management.

When entering the class of a master teacher, it is business as usual. The teacher engages each and every child in learning, and there is seldom a hint of poor student behavior. Working for nineteen years in a suburban high school as an administrator, reflecting back, over 90 percent of the teachers in a large public high school never wrote up a student for misbehavior in class. While conducting an observation or a brief walk-through, witnessing seamless, effective, and engaging bell-to-bell instruction was the norm.

There have been many books written regarding classroom management. Please refrain from reading any of them until you finish this book. The basic tenet of effective student management is being a consistent, honest, personable, respectful, caring individual who has developed his or her own style of teaching. Teachers need to be reflective practitioners who can look at their image in the mirror and constantly strive to be the best they can be. Poor student behavior is the direct result of the lack of an effective student-teacher relationship and poor teaching.

Teachers develop routines in their class to provide seamless instruction. The old expression "Idle hands are the devil's workshop" rings true when it comes to student engagement, management, and effective classroom routines.

Upon entry to the class, the students should be given a warm welcome and then understand that they need to engage in learning via a do-now activity, or as Madeline Hunter called it decades ago, the "anticipatory set." These expectations are developed with the students on the first day of class and the rules are established with student input, thus allowing the students to be a part of a decision-making activity and creating the culture of "their classroom." An experienced teacher possesses the ability to orchestrate this activity (Hunter, 1989).

Effective and engaging instruction trumps any opportunity for poor student behavior. However, there may be students in your class who enter your room with a history of making poor decisions and at times being disruptive. Effective instruction is one of the tools that will assist in dealing with these students.

The most important strategy that master teachers use in these situations is independent student management. Everyone in the faculty cafeteria has informed you that you will have your hands full, that that child will take all your energy and be a challenge every day. An important message for novice teachers to hear is that this problem will not go away—that child will be in your room every day—so let's work on strategies to make your class a special place for this particular student.

One short story that warrants sharing with you regarding student management involves a particular teacher, Mr. Jones, which is not his real name. He is a high school social studies teacher. One year he had a student in his class, Kyle (also not his real name), who we will say was a typical ninth-grade boy. If you have ever worked in a high school, you know the profile. He was also a member of the freshman football team.

Upon receipt of a discipline referral for this child from another teacher, our practice was to visit the student as soon as possible. During administrative rounds, planning to talk to Kyle, it was convenient to visit him during his social studies class with Mr. Jones. Upon me entering the room and requesting to speak with Kyle, Mr. Jones announced, "Kyle, my man, Dr. G. wants to talk with you." Mr. Jones also turned to me and stated, "Dr. G., Kyle is the man and we need him back as soon as possible—we were discussing something really important!"

This is how Mr. Jones operates: he identifies the neediest children and makes them part of the culture of the learning environment. The students are unaware that Mr. Jones has wrapped his arms around them and will provide them with the opportunity to be successful.

In speaking with Kyle, he said he was sorry and would apologize to the other teacher to work it out. As a seasoned administrator, one of my practices is to place the student in control of his destiny. This was accomplished by not assigning him detention or suspending him, but requiring him to work with another adult, the teacher who referred him, and build a relationship with her.

These are effective student management strategies that put students in control of their learning, allowing them to grow and make good decisions and become a productive member of their school community. He could have been punished using coercive disciplinary measures to isolate him, allowing him to develop anger and not trust the school administration. We need to work with students and allow them to grow and mature. The adolescent brain is not fully developed, and they will make poor decisions. Please allow them to grow!

Mr. Jones is one of the finest teachers and individuals in education today. The relationship he builds with every student is genuine, and he spends countless hours working with students over the hurdles of adolescence. Hopefully everyone reading this book has had a teacher like Mr. Jones; it is what pedagogy is all about. The message to novice teachers is build those special relationships with all your students and you will never have any student management issues.

TECHNOLOGY

Master teachers today incorporate technology into several aspects of their teaching. School districts are currently establishing communication venues that allow the teacher and student to be in contact 24/7. The use of school-based evaluation and instructional support programs—for example, at the university level, Blackboard—is very common and is the norm today in public schools. Parents can also view their child's progress on an ongoing basis and not have to wait until progress reports or report cards are distributed.

Teachers need to use technology in their day-to-day instruction. The use of technology, for example, Smart Boards and Elmos, are available to most teachers. Teachers need to be highly trained in this area, and it should be a major component in professional development activities throughout the year. The linking of instruction to the Internet is currently expected in the classroom. In addition, teachers need to use the Internet to provide engaging learning activities and enhance their instructional delivery.

The inclusion of game activities in the classroom makes learning interesting and fun. Let's look at one example: An elementary teacher is teaching addition and subtraction to second graders. All the teacher needs to do is Google "elementary math games for addition and subtraction"; there are several to choose from. Many of them are aligned with the Common Core State Standards, which provides the teacher with invaluable information regarding planning and documentation.

There are unlimited resources on the Internet available to teachers. Master teachers are constantly looking to enhance their instruction through the inclusion of technology. As mentioned earlier, this needs to be a major component in the professional development provided to all teachers.

Current technology also allows students to be exposed to people and activities around the globe, or with the school district next door, with a click of the mouse on their Chromebook. At Sacred Heart University in Fairfield, Connecticut, the College of Education just completed a pilot program between two neighboring school districts with drastically different socioeconomic demographics.

In order to break down racial barriers established by individual affluence and poverty, we connected students in the third and fourth grade to work on group projects on cultural heritage and immigration. Through the use of Chromebooks, Google Hangouts, and our newly developed website classeswithoutwalls.com, these students worked in groups of four to communicate face-to-face on various projects. If you wish to see the pilot program, log onto the website. More than one hundred students came to Sacred Heart University and presented their projects and enjoyed a day of celebration. This is just one example of the power of technology and teaching students twenty-first-century learning skills in the third and fourth grade!

The opportunities are endless.

2

E:
EMPATHY

Step into the Student's Shoes

If we were to look at our society at large, who are the most empathetic individuals we know? Who do many of us turn to during challenging times; who does one seek out for counsel when all else has failed? When there is a tragedy, who has that enduring personality that transcends all pain, anguish, and despair? Those individuals would be our religious leaders, those who have chosen a path in life to convey a religious message and serve.

The role of today's master teacher has drastically changed as it is the expectation that he or she be a caring and empathetic individual. Teachers work with diverse populations and must understand multiculturalism and be sensitive to the needs of each child (Cruz & Patterson, 2005). Students turn directly to those teachers whom they rely upon for emotional support and counsel, thus placing the teacher in a role that many educators are unaware of, something that is never discussed in their professional training, and something that is not reinforced in some school cultures. Those in the field of education who would disagree with this position are not master teachers.

If we look at memorable movies that highlighted a master teacher, several come to mind. In the original movie *The Karate Kid*, what role did Mr. Miyagi (Pat Morita) play in the life of Danny (Ralph Macchio), a transplanted adolescent, a child in a struggling single-parent family who faced social and emotional challenges (*Karate Kid*, 1984)? What role did Sean Maguire (Robin Williams) play in the life of Will Hunting (Matt Damon), a mathematical genius who struggled with his social and emotional being in *Good Will Hunting* (*Good Will Hunting*, 1997)?

The reason these movies were so successful and impactful lies in the fact that the adults assumed the role of the master teacher and mentor and forged everlasting relationships with their students to support them at times in ways that seemed unconventional. These are examples of master teachers understanding their students and empathizing with their personal situation.

So where does this place young teachers who have no idea how to balance the concept of empathy in their professional life? It is not easy. Many will ask themselves, *Where do I draw the line?* However, you must realize that if you are asking this question, you are not framing this concept correctly. Instinctively, we do many things without giving it any thought. We learn not to touch a hot stove, we know staring at the sun could damage our eyes, and we avoid situations that can cause us pain.

Empathy is no different; it has to come from the heart, be an instinctive response that is not thought about. Basically, the definition of empathy says it all: putting yourself in the place of others. Just think: How would you want to be treated?

When discussing this concept of empathy in graduate school, the response is incredible. Teachers and prospective teachers in many situations have never heard this in their studies. Teachers are inundated with state mandates, data, and professional performance indicators found on an Excel spreadsheet. However, think of that master teacher in our own personal lives—was he there for us, could we depend upon him to be supportive and nonjudgmental? These teachers really listened.

LISTENING

Teachers and students constantly engage in conversations throughout the day. The ability to build relationships with young people and guide them over the hurdles of childhood and adolescence is considered by many to be one of the most fascinating aspects of being a teacher.

There is no other profession (except religious leaders) that provides this opportunity.

The structure of our school environments, however, was originally designed from the factory model of the Industrial Revolution back in the early 1900s. At this time, placing hundreds, or even thousands, of students inside of four walls was a good idea. With the current trend toward smaller learning communities, educational leaders realize that smaller, more intimate environments are manageable and in many cases better support academic, social, and emotional growth.

If one were to stand in the hallway of a large, comprehensive high school during the change of classes, you would understand the trend to establish smaller learning communities. The collective energy of thousands of students can at times seem chaotic, confusing, and daunting. So once this confusion has settled into the classroom and the bell sounds, teachers are expected to perform, support each and every student in their class, and facilitate learning and individual growth. Teachers are also expected to be good listeners, possess the ability to sort conversations, and provide individual support for those who need it, whether it be academic, social, or emotional.

Master teachers fully understand the need to listen to their students. They find the time in this tumultuous environment to listen to their students in need. If you were asked to reflect upon specific traits of your favorite teacher, a majority of you would describe him or her as a good listener.

Once again, the need to do this must be instinctive. When a teacher feels that a student really needs to talk and is reaching out to him or her for help, this needs to become a priority. If this means that you may be late to a faculty meeting to spend time with a student in need, just do it. After the faculty meeting, explain to your administrators why you were late. If they challenge your decision, they need to read this chapter. Never, never leave a child in need of emotional support. If this causes a problem, it may be time to look for another school community where your personal commitment to each and every student is a priority.

CARING

The role of teachers has evolved greatly regarding caring for their students. The expectations of all constituent groups involved in education have placed this important aspect of schooling on the front burner. The easiest way for a new teacher to not receive tenure is to fall short in this area. The expectation, however, is for all professional and nonprofessional staff. The tenured teacher who starts to fall short in this area is sure to welcome some challenging moments from parents and administrators. In today's school communities, there are high expectations regarding how the adults care for their students.

The expected level of care that a student receives in school will be an ongoing discussion for years to come. A new teacher may ask, "What do you mean by 'care'?" One basic concept can guide teachers regarding the level of care they should provide for each and every student. That simple concept is, *How would I want* my *child to be treated?* If we base our actions on this simple concept, we will never fall short. All teachers need to remember this. Write it down in your plan book, and embrace the concept of caring for your students in a special way that they will always remember.

UNDERSTANDING THE INDIVIDUAL

One of the most exciting aspects of teaching is meeting so many young people. Who else has that opportunity to build relationships with young people on a yearly basis? The relationships that teachers build with their students are ever evolving, and we observe the students growing academically, emotionally, and socially. It is our job to support them over the hurdles of childhood and adolescence.

Although it may seem to be a daunting task, master teachers possess the ability to connect with their students and understand them as individuals. This is an unwavering commitment that the master teacher makes from the first day of class as a part of the educational experience of each and every child. This comes naturally and is inherent in the personalities of the teachers we remember.

There are always the individuals in public education who say that this is not possible. They bemoan, How can a high school math teacher who teaches 125 students a day get to know each student as an individual? With all the mandates and expectations being handed down, it is impossible for that teacher to be there for each and every child. There will always be those people Benjamin Franklin described as "immovable," but it is the teachers whom we remember who get it done, who make it a priority from day one.

Teaching is an extremely challenging occupation. Those who say that teachers have the summers off and they only work until 3:00 have no concept of what goes on behind the scenes of a teacher's daily workload. Master teachers commit their time to the students during school while they are in the building and after school on the stage or the playing field.

This will be called showtime. Whether it be in the classroom, on the athletic field, stopping by to have lunch in the student cafeteria with some of your students, sitting on an administrative assignment and giving extra help, counseling individuals during scheduled planning time, or attending an after-school event or game to support your students, the teachers we remember are always present. After all, it is showtime, and students, peers, administrators, and parents are watching.

These are personal and professional choices that teachers make. In today's schools, master teachers embrace the challenge and immerse themselves into the school life of their students. This is paramount in understanding all your students as individuals.

REMEMBERING THAT LIFE IS DIFFICULT

In the best seller *The Road Less Traveled* by M. Scott Peck, MD, the phrase "Life is difficult" introduces the text on page 1 (Peck, 2003). The purpose of this book is not to serve as a self-help book; however, at times we forget that life does get in the way. As a teacher, we need to always keep this in mind when we are dealing with all the individuals within the academic community. The connections and relationships that we establish with people evolve due to the concepts put forth in this text.

Let us not forget that there will be times when we need that additional support to make it through challenging times. The classic poem

"Footprints in the Sand" (Stevenson, 1939) should stay with all of us when we are helping someone in need.

The poem reminds us that at times we receive help and support from people to navigate the challenges of life. Master teachers wrap their arms around their students and provide them with this support, and the student is not even aware that this is occurring. This support is established through the genuine and authentic relationships that master teachers develop with their students. We have all had teachers in the past that have done this, and these are the individuals we remember and keep close to our hearts.

Remember, life is difficult and master teachers need to be there in a time of need.

LOVING

As a mother watches her child scurry off to the school bus for the first day of kindergarten, what is going through her mind? Her precious child is leaving her home, a safe little world, and entering the world of public education. Deep down inside, that mother is praying that the adults who will be working with her child will love him or her as much as she does and keep her child safe.

A parent's love for her child is unconditional, and cannot be matched by another individual. However, master teachers love their students as individuals and will always be there for them. In some cases, sad to say, the child may receive more love at school than at home. These situations are quite disturbing, and schools have acknowledged the fact that some children may have this void in their life. Support staff is always present to protect each and every child.

Hopefully this chapter of this book has opened your eyes, if you are a new teacher, to several characteristics that teachers need to possess in today's society. For the parents reading this text, understand that your child's master teachers have always possessed these traits and that this is an evolution and a reality that teachers entering the profession must adhere to.

This section on love is a culminating concept that has been discussed in this chapter titled "Empathy." Master teachers go out of their way to touch the hearts of their students and to be there with them forever:

> Teachers write on the hearts of their students
> Things the world will never erase.
> —Anonymous

In closing, at the end of the classic film *To Sir, with Love* starring Sidney Poitier as an out-of-work engineering student teaching in the East End of London in a challenging school environment, Lulu, a student, presents her teacher with a parting song. The message is quite powerful and summarizes several concepts discussed in this chapter. The strong connections that were developed and the life lessons taught by this teacher were embraced by these troubled teens and provided them with guidance to change their lives.

This occurs in the classroom of a master teacher. At the secondary level, the teacher is working with adolescents and young adults to assist them over the hurdles of life, which at times may seem daunting to the student. This form of love and care is an essential aspect of becoming a master teacher.

DEALING WITH LOSS

There are no school communities that are protected from loss; it is a part of life. When a parent, staff member, or student passes away, healthy school communities rally in support of those affected. Teachers and administrators are faced with the charge to stay composed and work with children and coworkers. This is not easy for some people, but that is okay. Teachers who share their emotions display the fact that they are human—it is okay to wear your heart on your sleeve. It is okay; the school will move forward and heal.

These situations may be extremely stressful to novice teachers. They will constantly ask, "How should we react? How do we help children when we are all grieving?" Professionals in the school building, that is, your psychologists and social workers, should conduct professional development activities to review protocols for how to deal with these horrific situations.

School communities deal with way too many situations of this nature. Parent loss, teacher loss, and student loss are experiences that every teacher would like to forget. But you can't, because it is part of your life as a teacher. One incident that occurred at North High School brought the school community to a screeching emotional halt when John passed away from mononucleosis.

School administration received the news at around 3:15 in the afternoon, and at that time the only students on campus were athletes. This was prior to Facebook and the instant access to media, so the challenge would be talking to six or seven teams about the loss of their dear friend. The memory of the school administrator approaching the cheerleaders is etched into his mind. When he was about ten feet away from them, Mary screamed and said "John, no!" He grabbed her as she started to collapse and was immediately surrounded by fifteen grieving teenage girls. With assistance, the administrators and coaches were able to get the girls to the guidance office and contact parents to drive them home.

The school community came together over the next several days with extensive counseling available to all, a midnight vigil, and the planting of a tree in memory of John. The school community had been wounded by this tragic event, and the scar will remain forever.

Unfortunately, all school communities experience many stories similar to the loss of John. Over time, schools experience student suicide, tragic car accidents, and death due to illness and violence. Schools need to have concrete procedures and plans to assemble crisis teams and bring in other mental health experts to help. Teachers need to get the message that the goal for the school that day is not to teach, but to support. Plans need to include areas where students can go to grieve and receive support.

All teachers are called upon to put on that other hat, and master teachers are able to support their students at every turn in the road. Be there for them.

STUDENT PROTEST: THE ULTIMATE TEACHABLE MOMENT

One might ask why this topic is in the chapter titled "Empathy." The reason students protest is because something is happening in the world that has profoundly affected them. On April 30, 1992, a high school community in East Harlem, New York, experienced a student walkout and protest over the Rodney King verdict.

By 9:00 on the above date, there were more than eight hundred students assembled on the front steps of the school, with a public-address system, voicing their frustration and anger over the verdict. And in Los Angeles, incidents relating to the verdict caused fifty-five people to lose their lives, more than two thousand people were injured, and a billion dollars in damage occurred in the wake of this verdict.

The fact of the matter was that the demographics of this public high school were 50 percent African American, 45 percent Latino, and 5 percent Asian. The professional staff was 95 percent white and the school was located in Harlem.

By communicating with student leaders early in the morning, school administration was able to organize a peaceful demonstration. The students felt respected and supported in their time of frustration.

The role of the master teacher is to keep the students safe, support them in their frustration, and listen. Master teachers who have their students' respect will turn this into the ultimate teachable moment, providing support and empathizing with their personal feelings. The goal of this day has changed: it is not a day to focus on instruction and having students take tests, it is a day of support. Situations of this nature are extremely stressful to all.

Some school administrators will see this as an act of defiance. They will feel that they have lost control of their building. They will revert to coercive measures and punishment for those who leave class to protest. These administrators will fail, and teachers who react in the same way will lose credibility with their students.

If we were to look back in recent history, we will see student protests that were handled by using coercive measures and imposing the school discipline code by school authorities. In 1992 there were proposed budget cuts to education in Florida. Several high schools and middle schools experienced student protests and walkouts over this decision. More than four hundred students were suspended for their participation in the protests.

In 2012, students at the Frederick Douglass Academy in Detroit walked out of classes to protest the education they were receiving. Among their complaints were the lack of consistent teachers, reassignment of the school principal, teacher abuse of sick time, and the shortage of textbooks. Approximately fifty students were suspended for their participation in the protest. The decision to respond with punitive action does not support the important concept of a teachable moment.

So what is the role of the teacher in incidents of this nature? Teachers need to listen, support, and contribute to the school community moving forward. Master teachers do not look toward administration and say to themselves, *How are we going to handle this?* All staff need to remain unified and deal with the situations that may become out of control. Make sure your students are safe, support one another, and continue to build that positive teacher-student relationship. Ask the school administrators if they need your help; it will not be forgotten by your school leadership team.

3

A:
ASSESSMENT

Monitoring Student Understanding and Progress

Assessment is a critical aspect of teaching that continues to be in the forefront of political agendas at both the state and federal level. The Race to the Top initiative placed student performance on the negotiating table as an essential component of the teacher evaluation systems across the country. In some districts, 50 percent of teachers' overall evaluation is based on the performance of their students on standardized tests.

Master teachers understand the law of the land and meet and surpass the expectations regarding student performance. This is done utilizing several assessment strategies that provide teachers with vital information regarding each and every student so the students can be provided with the tools to reach their potential and achieve success (Turner, 2014). In education, we have grouped assessment strategies into two categories: formative assessment and summative assessment.

When we look at the expectations of our teachers today and the day-to-day practices in the classroom, the area of formative assessment is extremely broad and undefined. Formative assessment is defined as all forms of assessing students outside of formal testing situations.

Summative assessment, on the other hand, is the quantitative analysis of a student on a standardized test or formal evaluation. Unfortunately, this is what drives education today and is in the forefront of political policy. The analysis of student performance data places an expectation on all of our teachers to achieve and exceed certain benchmarks.

The emphasis from the state departments of education to raise standards is not a bad thing, after all. How can we as educators condone lowering standards? State departments of education place expectations on their school districts and teachers to have their students perform on standardized evaluations, which one could argue is a result of effective teaching.

Herein lies the problem. The manner in which these expectations are conveyed to many teachers is counterproductive and places the teachers in a position of *teaching to the test*. Educators are under incredible pressure, causing the novice or new teachers to scramble to prepare their students for these standardized tests.

The solution is to have genuine and authentic learning happening in every classroom and to use formative assessment effectively to evaluate their students along the continuum of achieving their individual potential. Teachers need to have the academic freedom to utilize various instructional strategies and elicit higher-order thinking skills, thus providing their students with experiences that will far exceed the required skill set to perform well on standardized tests.

As mentioned earlier, formative assessment is broad and undefined and an integral part of pedagogy, thus providing teachers with the ability to develop an engaging and productive culture for learning in their classroom.

SUMMATIVE ASSESSMENT

One thing that we all need to realize is that summative assessment will never go away. It is here to stay. However, an emphasis on the formative assessment strategies introduced later in this chapter will establish a firm understanding of the wide range of assessment options and therefore alleviate some of the stress that is present in the formal testing environment. Whereas in some educational environments teachers feel that they need to teach to the test, we will discuss teaching beyond the test.

The wealth of knowledge presented in an array of engaging instructional activities will allow the students to look at summative assessment activities as a minimum or baseline level of understanding. If we look back at Bloom's taxonomy, the students will be involved in activities at the pinnacle of the triangle; analysis, synthesis, and evaluation, as opposed to the more basic concept of comprehension.

Master teachers always teach beyond the test and instill an overwhelming sense of confidence in their students that they will be successful. This is not a concept that is developed in an intense review session before a summative evaluation activity; rather, it is an ongoing belief and understanding that is established in the classroom culture from the first day of class. The initial message that a master teacher must deliver to his class is that all of his students will be successful and that together, they will find a way for that to happen.

The master teacher must declare that he will work with each and every student individually in order to make the success happen. This message is quite different from what some students hear year after year in their classes, but it is the resounding message in the classroom of a master teacher.

Some would agree that this is rather idealistic. Benjamin Franklin put individuals into three categories: those who are immovable, those who are movable, and those who move [people]. Individuals who frame these comments as being "idealistic" are either those who are movable or those who are immovable. Individuals who are movable will take the message being set forth in this text and run with it. They want to be a master teacher, and establishing a positive culture for learning where every child can succeed is a priority. As far as those who are immovable, we still hold out hope.

Wouldn't it be wonderful going to work every day and leading a charge where every child in your class will be happy and engaged and enjoy learning? Being exposed to that positive energy is exhilarating, and you will feel like you are not going to work. The expression "You have found the perfect job when you feel as if you never go to work" would ring true, and you would be at the helm of an incredible learning environment. This is the learning environment that allows all students to perform well on summative assessments. Teaching beyond the test is being done every day and has a long track record of success.

FORMATIVE ASSESSMENT

Where do we start? There is a litany of formative assessment strategies that a teacher can utilize on a daily basis. First and foremost, however, the use of assessment must not be coercive or punitive in nature. Assessment must be developmental and be used as an integral part of motivating students to achieve their potential. For example, how important is it that a freshman in high school understands the Pythagorean theory on October 22? If he doesn't understand it and fails a summative assessment, this grade will follow that student through his high school years and possibly affect the postsecondary opportunities that are available to him.

If he understands it on October 25, both the teacher and student are successful. This is one simple example where the opportunity for formative assessment to monitor student performance comes into play.

Here are some forms of formative assessment that are being used by teachers every day. The most important concept to remember regarding formative assessment is that in many cases it does not generate a *grade*: it provides the teacher with information regarding the student's understanding of a concept or specific information.

STUDENT JOURNALS

Teachers have utilized student journals for years before the advent of advanced technologies. Journals can be kept using the old-school "hard copy" method or maintained electronically. Some will argue that everything should be entered electronically, while others see the value of writing a journal, especially during the elementary years when writing skills are being developed.

The use of journal writing is limitless and can be used across all disciplines. Journal writing is an obvious instructional strategy in the humanities. Student-generated work within the confines of a journal provides the teacher with incredible insight into the students' understanding of the material and can allow students to reflect upon their learning experience. Journals can also be used in mathematics, where students can write down examples of a concept they learned and show examples.

This will provide affirmation that the student understands the concept and how he or she learned it, whether it is through instruction, classwork, homework, class game activities, or working with a friend. The use of journal writing encourages students to "write across all disciplines," an activity that is encouraged across several of the Common Core standards.

Journal writing also requires students to take ownership for their learning, a basic tenet of the work of William Glasser in *The Quality School*, as well as a driving force in the work of Charlotte Danielson. She often preaches placing the student in the center of the learning process (Glasser, 1999; Danielson, 2014).

GROUP ACTIVITIES

This instructional strategy has been introduced earlier in the techniques chapter of the text. However, there are specific aspects of this strategy that contribute greatly to the teacher's ability to assess a student's understanding of the topics being reviewed. Teacher observation of student interactions during group work is an invaluable formative assessment tool. This assessment strategy has been used for years by educators to collect information regarding the student's understanding of topics and concepts during a collaborative, student-centered learning activity.

The ability to evaluate in this collaborative venue, however, is not an easy or accurate way to evaluate individual student understanding. This strategy of formative evaluation is closely aligned to qualitative analysis, a research methodology used in advanced educational research that includes interviews, focus groups, observation, and other methods of collecting data without the use of numbers. Simply put, the teacher is observing the interaction of students and the participation and input that each student offers.

There are many other factors that come into play when you are observing group activities and are attempting to gather data regarding student understanding. Collaborative learning activities provide the opportunity for some students to excel and shine. This success is usually reserved for those outgoing, verbal students who are socially competent and confident.

There are the students, however, in the same group who are not interested or engaged in the learning activity and who are looking to just get by and collect credit for the group's accomplishments. The third group of students who are present in every classroom are those who are quiet and introverted and shy away from participating in the activity. These students may, or may not, have an understanding of the topics being discussed.

Therefore, you can understand how difficult it is to use the observation of group activities as a form of assessment. It does provide teachers with invaluable insight as to the learning styles of their students. These activities contribute to the culture for learning of the class, and the master teacher uses these strategies to support each and every student. Master teachers use the information collected from group activities to formatively assess their students as well as enhance the concept of individual student participation and student engagement in a collaborative learning activity.

STUDENT CLASSWORK

Throughout the instructional day, students are involved in a variety of learning activities. One effective instructional strategy is to provide students with time to work individually on concepts or problems presented in class. While students are working independently, the teacher has the opportunity to circulate throughout the class and observe the progress that each child is making.

After a short period of time, maybe two to three weeks into the semester, the teacher will establish an understanding of the individual learning styles and individual abilities of his students. If the teacher's instruction is satisfactory, then a majority of the students will grasp the concepts on a regular basis. (There may be an exception in remedial classrooms or working with students with learning disabilities; however, instruction should be modified to meet the needs of these students to be successful.) These students will be able to complete the classwork on a regular basis.

Some of the students may excel, which will require the teacher to differentiate instruction to challenge these students throughout the year. The most important aspect of this formative assessment strategy is that it provides invaluable information to the teacher to assist struggling students. The teacher observes students working independently and can assist and support them throughout the learning activity. The teacher can individualize instruction in the classroom setting and schedule additional time to work with students. This will support the notion that the teacher cares for the students and is willing to commit more time for the students to be successful.

This is what master teachers do in today's classroom.

BOARD WORK

One of the most effective and engaging formative assessment strategies is the participation of students in board work activities. This is especially true in the area of mathematics. When teachers are teaching mathematics, a common practice is to have a majority of the students place their solutions to problems on the whiteboard to share their accomplishments with the entire class.

Another common practice is to give each student a small whiteboard, and have them write down their solution at their desks and then share their work with the entire class. This would provide the students with a student-centered learning activity and promote student engagement. As for the students who wanted to just get by and go to their next class, there is no place to hide.

The one challenging aspect of involving students in these activities is to avoid embarrassing a student who does not know or understand the work being discussed. In this situation, teachers may have their students work with a partner to solve the problem on the board. This allows the master teacher to pair weaker students with stronger students, thus incorporating a cooperative learning strategy to ensure success and support for the weaker student.

Board work activities should be used in all disciplines. It places students in the center of the learning activity, and having them actively participate contributes to the culture of learning in the classroom, thus providing the teacher with invaluable assessment information.

HOMEWORK

The use of homework is a conversation in every school district across the country. Questions are thrown left and right: How much homework should be given by each teacher, how does it contribute to student learning, and how does the teacher use it as a formative assessment tool? Homework should be used to either provide the students with background information for an upcoming lesson, fulfill required reading in the humanities and literature, or reinforce concepts that were taught that day, thus providing the teacher with additional information regarding the students' understanding of the concept. The latter provides the teacher with valuable formative assessment information.

As previously mentioned, after a short period of time, the teacher is fully aware of which students need support. Some students who do well on a regular basis may have some minor misunderstandings, but the majority of the time their homework will be accurate and complete. Homework that is collected and reviewed will provide ongoing information regarding the struggling student.

Monitoring the students on an ongoing basis and providing appropriate intervention is critical for student success. Teachers who effectively monitor student progress and address individual deficiencies are preparing these students to be successful on summative assessment activities. When the students engage in classroom or state-mandated activities, the teacher should know how the student would perform.

Homework is one formative assessment strategy utilized by master teachers today.

EXTRA HELP

When teachers establish a positive culture for learning in their classroom, extra help is "cool." When students understand that not everyone grasps concepts immediately in class, and that after school the teacher will work with students to clarify certain concepts (and even provide some candy or snacks), going to extra help is a good thing. Teachers who explain to their class that they used to go to extra help supports the notion that it is okay. In addition, once the concept of students taking responsibility for their learning is prevalent in the learning culture of the class, students will attend extra help on a regular basis.

Learning after school is fun, social, and extremely collaborative. In these after-school sessions, everyone can take a deep breath and look at the problems at hand and work together. Earlier in the text we spoke about teachers always being there for their students to ensure success. This is just another example.

The formative assessment information collected during extra help sessions is invaluable. The teacher can work with the student to identify specific shortcomings and implement intervention strategies. These sessions provide the teacher with the opportunity to show the student that he really cares and wants him to succeed. It also creates a bond with the parents of the students. The teacher can keep the parents updated on their child's efforts and accomplishments, thus solidifying a bond between teacher, parent, and student. This bond is a critical component in supporting student success.

CLASSROOM GAME ACTIVITIES

Teachers can assess students' understanding through their participation in classroom game activities. These cooperative learning activities incorporate a high level of student involvement, competition, and fun, as well as contribute to a positive learning culture that teachers establish in their classrooms.

Having observed classroom game activities over the years like classroom Jeopardy! and Chemistry Island (scavenger hunt), were presented using PowerPoint. There are also many traditional classroom games (e.g., Bingo) that have been used for years.

Utilizing today's technology, teachers have access to web-based learning games that are engaging, interactive, and fun. If a first-grade teacher types in her browser "addition games," several fun, interactive games will appear. Many of these games are free and can be used to formatively assess students. These are new instructional strategies that teachers are implementing not only to enhance their instruction, but also to assess student understanding through a different medium. Some of these programs include:

Socrative

Kahoot
Zaption
Chatzy
Plickers

The use of this form of technology is definitely evolving in class-rooms across the country. Master teachers constantly update their in-structional strategies and seek out resources that can enhance their instruction. These programs can contribute greatly to the formative assessment strategies used in the classroom to support student learning. The use of this current technology has become a topic of conversation for the professional development of all teachers. These games are also aligned to the Common Core standards, thus enabling the teacher to include the activity to meet the instructional objectives of the lesson.

WEB-BASED POLLING ACTIVITIES

Similar to game activities, there are several programs accessible to all teachers to assess student understanding using questioning or polling activities. These polling sites can be fun and interactive in class. For example, in high school, instead of telling your students to put their cell phones away during class, have them take them out and log into "Poll Everywhere."

Interactive group instruction of this nature is available to anyone willing to put the time in to develop assessment strategies that are fun and engaging. These programs should be an integral part of profession-al development activities to enhance instruction and evaluation. The data received by these polling activities can provide invaluable data to inform future instruction and assessment.

ROLE-PLAYING

In several disciplines, role-playing is an instructional strategy that places students in the center of learning. It also requires students to take ownership of their learning and develop an in-depth understanding of the material. It also provides teachers with an opportunity to observe whether the students have grasped the concepts. This formative assessment strategy provides the teacher with invaluable insight as to student understanding and establishes a springboard to inform future instruction.

The humanities provide multiple opportunities to use role-playing as an instructional strategy. For example, world history students can conduct a session of English Parliament or reenact the Nuremberg trials. In English class, students can act out scenes from *Romeo and Juliet*. The teacher can observe these engaging learning activities, giving the students an opportunity to present their level of understanding of the instructional objectives.

QUESTIONING / SOCRATIC METHOD

Teachers rely heavily on the feedback that they receive during direct instruction through effective questioning strategies. Teachers are constantly honing their questioning strategies and techniques to provide effective instruction that elicits inquiry and higher-order thinking skills. All teachers should be encouraged to become highly efficient and effective in Socratic questioning and inquiry. The use of the Socratic method brings life and energy to the classroom. The students are engaged in ongoing, cyclical questioning activities that require higher-order thinking and inquiry. This provides teachers with invaluable information to be included in the formative assessment of a student.

It also allows the teacher to differentiate instruction to meet the individual needs of each student through well-planned and well-organized questioning sessions. Effective questioning techniques provide the teacher with critical information to inform additional academic support and intervention. Through early identification of student deficiencies, teachers can plan and organize support activities to allow their students to be successful and reach their potential.

EXIT SLIPS

Teachers should incorporate the use of exit slips as one of their strategies in their assessment arsenal. Exit slips provide an accurate account of individual student understanding at the end of a lesson. The inclusion of exit slips into the daily assessment of students is seamless and highly effective. As the students enter the class, you ask them to pick up an exit slip. This is a normal classroom routine that the students are familiar with. After the students are provided with the instructional summary at the end of class, the students then complete the exit slip.

The exit slip may be composed of a reflective question on the material or even an additional individual work of completing a math problem that they were working on earlier in class. As the students leave the classroom, they give the teachers their response on the exit slip. It only takes a few minutes for the teacher to review the exit slips and make a note as to which students are struggling. This will allow the teacher to follow up the next day and arrange to provide additional assistance to those targeted students.

PEER REVIEWS AND EVALUATION

Students bring a wealth of talent into the classroom that is not utilized in traditional teaching strategies, or school as we used to know it. The use of student input, review, and informal evaluation of a peer's work is powerful and establishes a positive and supportive connection between the members of the class. Although it sounds like an easy charge, it is not. Master teachers establish "rules of engagement" and stress that the input provided by their peers is "safe ground." The last thing that you would want to happen is having the student review process create friction between students.

This is an extremely powerful instructional and assessment tool. As mentioned earlier, the goal of effective instruction is to have students master concepts and ideas, and never create an environment that is coercive and punitive in nature. Assessment is the tool in which you quantify one's work, and understanding of a concept and utilizing peer input and evaluation frames this activity in a positive classroom culture for learning.

Peer reviews can be used in the evaluation of multiple learning venues and provide genuine and authentic feedback without any concern of affecting a student's grade. This is why, if set up properly, they are a powerful instructional tool.

STUDENT POTENTIAL

Many people believe that students possess a certain intellectual potential that correlates directly to their success in life. Many educators disagree. Whereas some students are more intellectually gifted than others, some students possess other qualities that will provide them with a strong foundation to be successful in any endeavor that they choose. The conversation regarding student potential is the focus of every parent-teacher conference, and every teacher must always look for each student to reach their potential.

The main concern is that as students move through twelve years of formal schooling, that is exactly what it is, formal schooling. Students are assessed using summative evaluations that leave little to the wide range of intelligences that an individual may possess.

Students move through the system and are categorized, as much as we may not like it, by their teachers and peers. This academic and social stigma is the result of putting hundreds of children together within four walls; it was bound to happen. Some students receive a stigma that is so strong, they will never be able to change and meet their potential.

The use of varied assessment strategies can help change this phenomenon. Providing the students a variety of venues where they can be successful will allow struggling students to transform into active and engaged learners, as opposed to being the daily class distraction or problematic student.

At the start of every new school year, all students are given a fresh start. Master teachers speak with the past teachers of struggling students and find out what worked and what did not. They develop plans to support that child and make them successful from the first day of class. This is what master teachers do: they look out for the well-being of every student.

4

C:
CONTENT

Your Academic Discipline

Mastering the content of one's discipline is a basic tenet of being a master teacher. Teachers are trained in certain disciplines and participate in teacher preparation programs that provide them with a solid foundation to enter the world of pedagogy (Shing, Saat, & Loke, 2015). Master teachers realize that this world is quite unique, challenging, and rewarding.

Teacher preparation programs are all monitored by state and federal agencies to ensure that they meet certain standards and are providing teacher candidates with the proper foundation for success. Some students participate in four-year teacher preparation programs while others, like career changers, participate in graduate programs that provide a faster track to teacher certification. One concern regarding these faster-paced graduate programs is the amount of content that is being transferred from their undergraduate programs and whether additional coursework can be delivered in a relatively short period of time.

All teachers have two invaluable resources to level the playing field in regard to content: the Internet and the Common Core State Standards. To put this in perspective, thirty years ago the only person who knew algebra was the teacher and all the information was contained in the textbook.

Today, at the click of a mouse you can access hundreds, maybe even thousands, of resources explaining concepts in algebra, watch instructional videos, and find the complete list of Common Core standards that teachers across the country use every day in their classrooms. All the content for every discipline is contained in the Common Core standards. Therefore, all teacher candidates can access this information and be completely current regarding their area of expertise.

UNDERSTANDING THE COMMON CORE

Teachers choose a discipline and are trained to be an expert in that field of study. Once a teacher completes educational preparation programs and secures a position, he or she needs to fully embrace the Common Core State Standards Curriculum. Teachers should make it a priority to have the Common Core at their fingertips as it contains all the standards that they will be expected to include in all the day-to-day lessons.

When the Common Core arrived on the educational horizon, it was met with some resistance from educators who were experienced and successful in their schools. The Common Core was initially viewed by many as yet another federal mandate and was not aligned to their current curriculum guides. In most cases, however, the Common Core simply reworded what was currently being taught in our schools. The Common Core was developed by educators across the country and was focused on developing common standards across all school districts. So in the beginning many kicked and screamed, but everyone eventually adopted the standards.

An analogy can be made if we compare teaching to the medical profession. If we become ill, medical professionals have a common practice and prescription to cure your illness. If you have bronchitis, the doctor will probably prescribe a Z-Pak and send you on your way. If you are diagnosed with diabetes, you will most likely be prescribed a regimen of metformin as an initial intervention.

So if you are a third-grade teacher and you are studying the economy and manufacturing in your home state, your unit may include seeking out information via the Internet, class handouts, and selected texts. The activities presented during the unit would address the following Common Core standards, to name a few:

- CCSS.ELA-LITERACY.RI.3.1: Ask and answer questions to demonstrate the understanding of a text, referring explicitly to the text as the basis for the answers.
- CCSS.ELA-LITERACY.RI.3.2: Determine the main idea of a text, recount the key details and explain how they support the main idea.
- CCSS.ELA-LITERACY.RI.3.2: Use text features and search tools (e.g., key words, sidebars, hyperlinks) to locate information relevant to a given topic efficiently (The Common Core Standards).

Master teachers realize how much information they have at their fingertips. The Common Core standards provide a road map of objectives that provide consistency and detail. The Common Core should never trump academic freedom; rather, it should serve as a guide along the continuum of a specific discipline.

CURRICULAR EXPERTISE

The content for one's discipline is woven into the curriculum developed in every school system across the country. Curriculum committees or academic departments also have resources from their state education departments regarding curricula and certain guidelines that should be used while developing curricula.

Once the school has adopted a curriculum, which is usually done in collaboration with the teachers of that discipline, it is the role of the teacher to deliver. The teachers who participate in the development of a curriculum usually have some level of curricular expertise, which contributes to and helps shape the curriculum adopted by a school or district.

There is only one way to become an expert in curriculum: immerse yourself and practice it every day. One beautiful aspect of teaching is taking the curriculum and making it your own. Master teachers enjoy the academic freedom to incorporate a variety of teaching methodologies to provide their students with an engaging and exciting educational experience. Curricular expertise comes with time, and master teachers are always looking to improve and modify their delivery of the curriculum.

GLOBAL INITIATIVES

The best-selling book *The World Is Flat* by Thomas Friedman (Friedman, 2005) highlights global perspectives of how the world is changing. He discusses the radical changes in world economics, politics, and how our world has become flat. Students who enter the workforce after sixteen years of formal schooling need to experience how the world has changed and understand the global nature of their everyday life.

For example, if you go to the emergency room in a hospital on a Sunday night with a broken leg, the technician will take several x-rays to determine the severity of your injury. You will sit in the treatment room waiting for the results and see very few people; after all, it is Sunday night. When you ask who is reviewing your x-rays, the nurse informs you that they are being reviewed by technicians in India!

When you call customer service for your phone company or a major department store, haven't you noticed a different accent? Outsourcing is just one global initiative used today by large corporations. Master teachers incorporate global learning initiatives in their classrooms.

The use of technology allows educators to communicate with individuals around the world at the click of a mouse, view the world through the thousands of webcams set up around the globe, and expose their students to global learning and experiences. The learning environment needs to be expanded outside of the four walls of the classroom to prepare our students for the adult world that they will be entering after graduation.

EFFECTIVE PLANNING

Unit and lesson planning is essential to provide the students with an effective learning experience. New teachers are overwhelmed with the amount of time required to plan an effective lesson due to the basic requirements: establishment of student learning objectives, providing engaging and effective learning activities, planning effective assessment strategies, differentiating to meet the needs of individual students, placing the student in the center of the learning process, and recording student outcomes.

It is mandatory that specific Common Core standards be noted in every lesson plan. The objectives of the lesson need to be aligned to these standards in order to organize daily lesson plans and provide proper sequencing throughout the units. Year after year, the master teacher organizes instruction and makes changes to ensure that the needs of the students are being met.

CHILD DEVELOPMENT

Student performance on standardized tests has clearly become the focus of our educational systems, as well as teacher evaluation systems, across the country today—and school administrators and teachers are being held accountable. In order for our students to be successful, however, we forget at times that we are dealing with children, not drones or machines that we can build and guarantee that each one will be the same. As mentioned earlier, if innovative and engaging learning activities are implemented in the classroom, the students will far exceed the minimal standards set forth by state assessment systems.

The understanding of child development is at times lost or placed on the back burner in our day-to-day experience with children. It is rather interesting that we expect adult behaviors from individuals whose brains are not fully developed, whose physiological change and growth is ongoing, and whose hormonal rage is exploding.

In any given classroom, you can have children whose ages span several years. For example, in first grade, you can have a child who is five years old sitting next to a child who is seven. Considering that the one student has experienced an additional two years of growth, why are the expectations the same for both students? As these children continue through their schooling years and enter adolescence, the age difference continues to have implications regarding academic, social, and emotional growth. How often do teachers base their expectations on the chronological age of the student?

It is imperative that teachers understand the different stages of child development. These considerations need to be part of the academic, social, and emotional expectations for the individual student. When meeting with parents during conferences, this needs to be a topic of discussion.

A LIFELONG LEARNER

Whenever we go to the doctor for an examination or procedure, we want to receive the best medical care available. Imagine going to a doctor who uses medical procedures from ten or twenty years ago! I am quite sure that this medical professional would no longer have a medical practice.

Master teachers remain current with new and innovative teaching strategies to provide the most effective learning environment for their students. If a teacher stands in front of the class for forty-five minutes and lectures, you can be assured that that teacher will be placed on a professional growth plan to enhance his or her instruction through the implementation of innovative teaching strategies. Teachers need to model the concept of being a lifelong learner. Individual growth and personal learning occurs with every experience, whether it is a formal activity or sitting and talking with a child and helping the child deal with a personal situation. We learn from each other every day.

Professional development activities should expose teachers to innovative strategies that will enhance instruction. These programs are ongoing, year after year, and engage teachers in professional learning communities. After the professional development activities, however, it is the responsibility of the teacher to implement these new strategies. Your master teachers will immediately incorporate these new initiatives in their instruction, whereas your less effective teachers will not change and revert back to their antiquated practices.

5

H:
HUMOR

Making Minds Smile

Is humor that important?

Students must be motivated to learn. When we look at the day in the life of a student, the student is subjected to several learning activities that address a variety of disciplines. High school students, for example, sit through five or six classes and are exposed to what we call a liberal education. These experiences provide a broad foundation of knowledge, something we have all survived.

Do you think it would be challenging to go through the school day of a typical high school student? It is long, tedious, frustrating, challenging, and sometimes unmanageable. Do students really look forward to sitting in a chair and at times learning something that they question if they will ever need? Students are generally compliant and fulfill their role. It is the established system of public education.

We all remember those teachers who had a keen wit and sense of humor (Strean, 2008). We recall those classes as being a "breath of fresh air" during a physically and mentally draining and stifling day. Students need to be motivated to learn, and master teachers weave humor into the fabric of their instruction.

AUTHENTICITY

It is important, however, that the humor you infuse into your daily interactions with your students is authentic. This is one of the aspects of style, discussed in chapter 8 in this book, that allows every teacher to put a personal touch to their instruction. Whereas we can observe master teachers and their use of humor, it needs to be from the heart. Every teacher is somewhat "funny" at some time during the day. Whether it be talking to our friends, our spouse, or our significant other, we are all blessed with a sense of humor. All teachers need to identify their humor, cultivate it, and weave it into their personal fabric of instruction.

Students are attracted to different forms of humor, so there is no real answer to what it looks like. From the first day of class, you begin this journey of countless interactions with so many different individuals providing you with an opportunity to use humor to show your students that you are human. We all experienced twelve formal years of schooling, where a majority of the teachers rarely cracked a smile. It was business as usual. They were teachers, not real people. When you saw them outside of the classroom you would completely change back to that passive learner sitting and listening to their lectures.

Thankfully, today master teachers are like pied pipers. When students see you in the community, they greet you and are excited to see you. They say to their parents, "There's Mr. Johnson!" Many times the parents will approach you to say how much they appreciate the work you are doing with their child.

BALANCE

Whereas humor is an important component to a healthy culture for learning, it needs to be balanced with the seriousness of academic rigor. Classroom environments need to focus on business as usual—What are the goals and the standards we are going to meet today?—and a specific plan must be in place to meet those goals. As previously mentioned, classrooms have become engaging environments where students come to class looking forward to learning and being the audience for the teacher's professional performance.

The master teacher understands this and is able to weave humor into every lesson and still meet the lofty goals that support rigor. We all need to realize that teaching is an innate talent that cannot be taught in an education class. Watching a master teacher in front of students—to witness the special bond, the engaging conversations, and the personalized humor used to motivate them—is a quite unique and incredible experience.

MOTIVATION

Humor in the classroom is an ongoing form of motivation that comes naturally to the master teacher. The typical school day for a high school student is long, tedious, frustrating, and challenging. So why are we surprised when students act out and misbehave? Traditional education had the student sitting in front of a teacher, being exposed to low-level clerical duties, copying down notes, and occasionally being asked a question. Thankfully, this is no longer the case.

Master teachers have students walking into their rooms with an anticipation that learning will be fun, engaging, challenging, and motivating. Along with the nature of the activities that are designed to motivate the students, humor is effectively used to motivate our students to want to learn. We all remember those teachers who had this gift: the ability to keep us focused and engaged for the entire lesson.

Many students, after the first day of school, no matter what grade, cannot wait to describe to their parents one or two of their teachers who are really funny and cool. This happens every year, and the sharing of the stories while having dinner or driving to an after-school activity creates the powerful bond between student, parent, and teacher.

Teachers need to understand the impact they have on their students. Motivating instruction with appropriate humor will have your students running to your class and talking about you all over town. You will be the main topic of conversation in the produce aisle of your supermarket, on the sidelines of a soccer game, and at the local nail salon.

6

E:
ENERGY

Leading a Positive Culture for Learning

What does it look like?

Master teachers immerse themselves in the learning environment every day. Teaching is not a job or a career; it is a way of life. The energy that a teacher brings to the classroom can take on many forms. It depends on the individual teacher. All master teachers have carefully honed their teaching style to utilize the personal energy that they bring to the classroom (Säfström, 2014).

We have all experienced a wide range of teaching styles in our educational experience, whether it be in the elementary grades, secondary school, or in postsecondary studies. As individuals we tend to favor certain teaching styles that appeal to us, but we can always acknowledge the positive energy that a teacher brings into the classroom. Sitting at our desks, we witness the energy that a master teacher possesses and conveys to each and every student.

It doesn't matter if the student is an overachiever or a struggling student, the energy is real and apparent. Master teachers look at every class as game time. There are no cheers or loud celebrations, but as the teacher you are focused and you are seconds away from creating a masterpiece.

This energy is embodied in the master teacher; it is nothing that can be learned or included in a presentation, or even be taught by a professor with an advanced degree.

It is the responsibility of teacher preparation programs to strike this burning ember inside of teacher education candidates and lead them down the path of accessing the energy that lies within. Young adults possess endless energy and potential, and is the responsibility of the professor to start each and every student down the road of pedagogy with passion and energy at the forefront.

At times, professors tend to believe that they are too important—just remember that basically the only difference is that they are more educated and experienced. To educate means to lead, so lead each and every candidate down the path to find their inner energy and passion for pedagogy.

POWERFUL AND UNDERLYING

As human beings, our individual potential is endless. Many of us do not realize that within us all lies the opportunity to make a difference in this world. There are many reasons why we tend to be stifled and feel limited; whether it be by internal or external forces, it happens to all of us. Teachers need to understand the power of their underlying energy. Take another look in the mirror, do not cheat the man or woman in the glass, and go for it.

Teaching and preaching the following concept is critical: unleash that potential and make a difference every day in your classroom. Teachers become bogged down with mandates and distractions, but do not let this divert you from your mission. If you move forward and make this your main focus, the distractions will disappear because you will be the finest teacher in your school.

TWENTY-SEVEN THOUSAND

The number *twenty-seven thousand* presents an important concept that all teachers must understand and embrace. A typical school year involves at least 180 days of instruction. High school teachers teach five classes a day. That is nine hundred lessons a year. If you calculate how many lessons a teacher teaches over a thirty-year career, that is twenty-seven thousand performances. The amount of energy expended over a lifetime of teaching is mind boggling. This is why teaching is not a job or a career, it is a way of life.

This is why master teachers have found the perfect job; they never feel as if they are going to work. Every day brings new and exciting experiences and interactions with hundreds of people. The positive energy that teachers bring to the classroom cannot be taught. It is innate and who they are. It is fascinating to observe the different forms of energy that teachers bring to the classroom.

Some teachers are showmen, where every class is a workout, passing all of that energy to each individual student, whereas others are calm and methodical, infusing energy through their warm and inviting personality and ensuring that their concern for each student is genuine. These are just two examples of how master teachers possess this gift and offer it to their students every day.

CREATING THE MASTERPIECE

There are very few occupations that allow you to create five master-pieces a day. Effective teachers reflect back on every lesson as a master-piece, and are proud of the learning experiences they provided to their students. Many of us played sports or competed in our lives; teaching is no different—every lesson is game day. Teachers carefully control the adrenaline rush before every class and use their unique pedagogical style to provide the students with a masterpiece.

As mentioned earlier, this takes extensive planning and thought and does not come easily to the novice teacher. In fact, these lessons can be extremely challenging and stressful to new teachers who are looking to be perfect from the first day of class and impress their school administration and colleagues. As a new teacher, you will not be perfect. You will have your successes and your failures, rewards and challenges, and every day you will take steps along the continuum of becoming a master teacher.

Students look forward to an engaging and exciting lesson, and the energy that they bring into the room will contribute to the positive culture for learning that has been established in the class. Teachers understand that students are an integral part of creating this master-piece, and the learner, along with the educator, travels down the path of learning, creating, and being a participant in the masterpiece.

PASSION FOR YOUR DISCIPLINE

The energy that master teachers bring to their classroom is partially embedded in their passion for their discipline. Teachers need to love what they teach. It only takes a few minutes of watching a teacher in the room to understand this concept; their discipline is part of who they are. The teaching profession is quite unique in that teachers live their lives always being a teacher.

You will see teachers outside of the classroom at social events, and if the opportunity arises, they catapult themselves into teaching mode. They find themselves falling into the teacher trap, attending a family function and talking to the kids about science, creating a little informal classroom away from their classroom.

This is why it takes a special person to become a teacher. Individuals who enter teacher preparation programs need to have this innate pas-sion to become a master teacher. Individuals who enter the profession for other reasons usually fail or become frustrated and struggle throughout their career. If you identify yourself as one of these individ-uals, please, do yourself, your school, and your children a favor: please find another career.

When we visit our doctors, we want them to be passionate about their medical career, wanting to take care of us in the best way possible. We want them to understand and fully embrace their discipline, medi-cine. When the parent of a first-grade teacher drops his child off at school, there is the same expectation. Parents place their children into the hands of professional educators, and they expect that their children will be participants in a wonderful learning experience, and quite frank-ly, they should expect nothing less.

PASSION FOR PEDAGOGY

Equally important as having a passion for your discipline is having a passion for pedagogy. The definition of pedagogy, the "teaching of children," at times is placed on the back burner when we are attending staff development activities or addressing initiatives set forth by our school or district. You have to love children if you are going to become a master teacher.

The choice to use the word *passion* is obvious, because this is what needs to get you up in the morning. Elementary school children in general are excited about school, a place that is engaging, invigorating, and rewarding. Teachers need to feel the same energy as they are driving to work. As they make their commute, they should be thinking about how many lives they can touch today and how they can make a difference in the life of a child.

Once again, this is something that cannot be taught; it needs to be who you are. The most important time in a teacher's day is the ride home from work, the time when he can reflect, thinking about how he supported the growth of every child in his class. Upon their arrival home, all teachers should look at the person in the mirror and reflect. The author of the poem "The Guy in the Glass" (Wimbrow, 1934) asks you to do the same thing. You need to be honest with yourself and think about how you impacted the life of every student you worked with that day. You may realize that you made a mistake, and that is quite common; we are all human.

The power of reflection needs to drive the master teacher toward perfection, which should be the goal of every teacher. If you are lying to the person in the mirror, you will fail.

Pedagogy, the art of teaching children, must be what gets you up in the morning.

7

R:
RELATIONSHIPS

Creating That Special Bond

The establishment of positive relationships with every child in your class is probably the most important aspect of teaching. Master teachers understand that there needs to be a special bond between teacher and student, and this is something that they work on from the first day of class. If we look back, these are the teachers we remember, the ones who took that extra time to talk with us, attended our wrestling match or dance recital, or spent a weekend on a school retreat or community service activity. Beginning teachers need to understand this and work on building positive relationships with each and every child (Mester, Spruill, Giani, Morote, & Inserra, 2015).

Unfortunately, teachers at times get caught up in mandates and initiatives that either distract them or limit the time that they can commit to working on this critical aspect of pedagogy.

RAISING THE CHILD

In Hillary Clinton's best seller *It Takes a Village*, the message is loud and clear: every adult involved in a child's life is expected to provide support and guidance. Every adult has an impact on the life of a child. "Every adult" means family members, members of the community, religious leaders, friends, and teachers. A fact that few of us realize is that in our society today where both parents may be working or children may come from a single-parent family, those children spend more time in school than at home and have more contact with school personnel than their parents. Therefore, who is raising the child?

All adults in our learning communities need to understand this. This does not only include teachers, it involves all individuals in the school setting, and for most children their school day starts and ends with the bus driver. All adults in schools are teachers; whether it be the staff in the main office, the custodians, or the playground monitors, we all accept and assume a role as teacher and mentor. It does not only pertain to the professional staff that includes teachers and support personnel.

Teachers need to look back at their years of public education and teaching and realize that the lifelong relationships established with the students are probably the most rewarding aspect of one's professional career. Seeing a parent in the grocery store and asking about her child, reflecting back on the high school years with a former student, or meeting a student from years ago and his new family is incredibly rewarding. After these encounters, teachers drive away clearly understanding that they made a difference and helped raise that child into the person he has become. Hopefully the positive and supportive relationships will have an impact on how our students will raise future generations.

At times, educators forget that they are in a "human" business. All educators can fall into the trap of mandates and school-wide initiatives that at times distract them from building a powerful relationship with each and every child. Master teachers engage with students throughout the school day and participate in "raising" every child.

COMMUNICATION

The establishment of effective relationships requires open and ongoing communication. Teachers need to understand that in today's world they are expected to communicate on a regular basis. All teachers, however, are encouraged to engage as much as possible in the traditional mode of communication: face-to-face conversations.

Students today are so immersed in the world of social media that there is little face-to-face communication, even with their friends. How often do we walk past a cafeteria table full of students, and while none of them are talking, they all are texting? Yes, it is important to engage in effective e-mail conversations today; however, take the time to sit down and talk. These are the moments that students will remember and parents will appreciate the fact that you took time out of your day to help raise their child.

Teachers have an exclusive opportunity to personally engage with students. We are trained professionals in the field of education and child development, unlike anyone else in the child's life. Educated working parents may be very successful and intelligent, but they are not trained in the art of pedagogy. Parents also assume a certain role in their child's life that is quite different from that of a teacher in many ways; however, there are also many similarities. Teachers are considered "in loco parentis." They are to assume the role of a parent while the child is in school. Teachers have an incredible status in the eyes of a child and need to understand that they have an amazing influence on their students. This is why it is imperative that teachers constantly personally communicate with their students to guide them through all aspects of their life during the years that they attend school.

AUTHENTICITY

Students in our public schools are very smart. They possess an innate sense as to whether your concern and care for them is genuine and authentic. This holds true for students from kindergarten through twelfth grade. Simply put, they can always detect a "phony."

Students communicate their resentment to a teacher in a variety of ways. In the elementary years when certain social filters are not yet developed, they may just say, "You really don't care about me." In the later years, students will be disruptive, show a lack of respect for the teacher, or disengage from learning, which contributes to a poor culture for learning in the classroom. Unfortunately, we all remember these inauthentic teachers too well.

One of the main reasons that individuals enter the teaching profession is because of their experience in their schooling years. There was that teacher, or hopefully several, who were genuine and authentic, inspiring a young mind to look at the world differently and walk beside them. These individuals made lifelong impressions that one will never forget and will impact the lives of many, many that they will never meet.

This is clearly an attribute of a master teacher that cannot be taught; it is innate and powerful. Individuals who do not possess this quality will not enjoy the teaching profession; they will struggle at work and possibly eventually fail. Unfortunately, many students will be shortchanged along the way.

Imagine if you felt that your religious leader was not authentic and genuine. Where would that leave you regarding your faith in your religion and the support that you look for when you are in need? Teaching is no different.

LIFELONG IMPRESSION

The greatest outcome of being a master teacher is the impact that you will have on the lives of your students long after their schooling years. We all remember those special teachers and the impression that they made on our lives. At times we will not even realize how they contributed to the individuals that we have become. We look up to these individuals and understand that they helped shape the people we have become, and at times we look back at our experiences for guidance and direction.

The master teachers make an impact not only on the students they teach, but everyone those students come into contact with during the course of their lives. The respect, admiration, and life lessons that you taught will guide all your students to better life decisions and affect the way they will raise their children and the way they interact with their grandchildren.

One of the most moving motion picture scenes that reflects the impact of a master teacher or role model was at the end of the movie *Saving Private Ryan* (*Saving Private Ryan*, 1998). If you do not know the story, a squad of soldiers were sent to save Private Ryan (Matt Damon) because his other three brothers were recently killed in combat. This is a policy that the army put in place to save a last surviving child.

Captain Miller (Tom Hanks), who was an English teacher before being drafted, is dying in battle, and he says to Private Ryan, "James, earn this, earn it," meaning, earn the sacrifice that these soldiers have given to save your life. Then the movie fast-forwards to Private Ryan, at the time probably in his seventies or eighties, at the grave of Captain Miller at Arlington Cemetery. The grave of the man who rescued him and taught him powerful life lessons had a profound impact in a short period of time. The elderly Private Ryan asks his wife, with tears in his eyes, to "tell me I've led a good life."

Master teachers may not have an impact as powerful as this example, but students remember the guidance, support, and wisdom for years after leaving your classroom.

Another powerful image that comes to mind is the impact that Erin Gruwell had on students living in an inner-city environment in the movie *Freedom Writers* (*Freedom Writers*, 2007). This young, inexperienced teacher possessed the ability to redirect the anger of these impoverished students and create a movement that has saved the lives of countless students living in poverty and given them hope and opportunity to live a better life.

These young adults will remember their teachers who pushed and prodded them to become involved in the Freedom Writers Foundation, opening up opportunities to attend college and drastically change the course of their lives.

8

S:
STYLE

A Unique, Personal Approach

To provide closure and complete the concept of the master teacher today, this chapter of the book is critical. When we look back at our school experiences, we always remember those master teachers and their style. It was just something about their personality and mastery of teaching that we will never forget.

Style is personal and includes several of the concepts previously mentioned. We all like to select our own wardrobe, choose a certain model of a car, decorate our homes in a certain way, and engage in certain activities in our lives. One of the greatest characteristics of our education system is that the students will be exposed to various individual styles and this will allow them to develop into their own individual person.

The concept of style in teaching goes way beyond the physical and outward appearance. No teacher in any education class or any school administrator can teach you the concept of style. New teachers are concerned about their overall image and how they are perceived by others. At times they will revert back to the style of their favorite teacher and try to emulate their personality. Yes, we clearly learn from master teachers we have learned from in the past, but you need to craft your own personal style (Higgins-D'Alessandro, 2002). You obviously need to stay inside the lines and always comport yourselves in a professional manner, which is an expectation of all educated professionals.

Students love being exposed to a variety of individual styles during the course of the school day. It is what makes learning fun and exciting.

APPEARANCE

Teaching is a profession. When it is all said and done, you have gone through more years of schooling than any lawyer and if you pursue your doctorate, you are probably close to the years of school that a medical doctor is required to complete.

Young teachers must strive to become a master teacher and portray the correct image to their school community. How would you feel if you went to see a doctor, lawyer, or accountant and he or she had on ripped jeans, a Grateful Dead T-shirt, full body tattoos, and extensive piercings? If teachers want to be considered professionals, they should present a professional appearance. This advice is for all teachers, but it is critical for young teachers entering the field and looking to secure a teaching position. Anything in moderation is somewhat acceptable so please keep this in mind. Remember that you have a profound impact on your students.

The individual style of teachers is also reflected in their attire. Some school leaders will settle for nothing less than a shirt and tie for male teachers and, for female teachers, a skirt or business attire. This is an excellent image but it is not a requirement. For men, minimally you should wear business casual or "the uniform": neat khakis and a collared shirt. A sport coat is optional, but it does send a professional message. For the ladies, dressing conservatively is critically important. Please use good judgment.

Teaching positions are highly competitive, and you always want to position yourself at the top of the list. You need to remember you are a professional and you will be judged on your appearance.

PERSONALITY

Teaching is probably one of the most rewarding professions in society today. It is a way of life that allows individuals to make contributions to their school and society. In this role, teachers have the opportunity to infuse their personality in their day-to-day teaching. School districts that have healthy school cultures embrace academic freedom for their teachers, allowing them to reach their goals using varied instructional practices and encouraging them to develop their own personal style of teaching and working with students.

Effective administrators make this a part of the ongoing conversation they have with all teachers, especially those starting their career. Novice teachers should come to work with the anticipation of making a difference in the lives of children and looking forward to creating their craft and their own personal style of teaching. As a teacher drives to work, she should be excited to see her students. Her adrenaline should be flowing just like an athlete before a game. Teaching is not a job or a career; it is a way of life!

GENUINENESS

As mentioned earlier during the chapters titled "Empathy" and "Humor," a teacher's style needs to be genuine. You will be influenced by instructors in your education programs and possibly influenced by administrators when you first start teaching, but remember, no one can teach you your style of teaching. If you choose to emulate the styles of other professionals, you will fail. You will struggle every day and teaching will present itself as a job.

Master teachers embrace the fact that their style is genuine. One of the most enjoyable parts of an administrator's day is circulating throughout the classrooms and observing so many different styles of teaching.

The final story regarding style is powerful and memorable. Mr. Mike Johnson, an excellent chemistry teacher in one of the most successful science research programs in the country, exhibited his "style" during an observation.

While observing his chemistry class, Mr. Johnson surprised his class with a special treat: he had purchased a ventriloquist dummy as an instructional tool. The dummy was dressed in a blue shirt and khakis with a tie that had elements on it. Typical chemistry teacher. In addition, Mr. Johnson had on the exact same outfit. Mr. Johnson had no right using a ventriloquist dummy. He was horrible at it; his mouth moved and his attempts were always done with a smile and chuckle.

Effective administrators are always looking to get involved in the lesson; therefore, during one of the question-and-answer sessions, Mr. Johnson called upon the administrator to respond. The administrator had taken chemistry over three decades ago, so it was inevitable that the response would be incorrect. This was a setup for failure! Immediately, without hesitation, the dummy shouted out, "Ah ha, looks who's the dummy now!" The class immediately turned and looked for a reaction from the administrator. After the administrator became hysterical, the entire class became unglued with laughter.

At the end of the lesson, the administrator commented sternly, "Mr. Johnson, stop by later after school. As for your little friend, we can find him a woodpile." Once again, the class became hysterical. After congratulating Mr. Johnson with a high five, the administrator gave the dummy a loving slap in the head while leaving the classroom.

Mr. Johnson has always looked to making his instruction fun and engaging. The purchasing of a ventriloquist dummy and actually trying to use it provides instruction infused with humor and his own personal style.

The master teacher with a sense of humor and a personal style that consumes a room. Kudos, Mr. Johnson!

This is such an exciting way of life. To work with children and young adults is a blessing, so enjoy every minute and charm them with your genuine style of teaching. It is an experience that they will remember for a lifetime.

BEING COMFORTABLE WITH WHO YOU ARE

Let's face it: you are going to be nervous when you first start teaching. You already may be wondering, *How am I going to become the master teacher described in this text?* You need to be able to be reflective and look at yourself in the mirror every day, being confident that you are going to do the best for every student you encounter. You will be faced with situations that you are unclear as to how you should handle it. Master teachers deal with these situations without hesitation or thought; it comes naturally to them.

If you look at yourself as a caring and dedicated teacher looking to make a difference, you will not fail. If you follow the guidance of this text and research certain aspects of a master teacher noted in this book, it will only give you more of an in-depth insight as to the importance of that trait. Read this book with a laptop nearby. If something impacts you immediately, research it. There is no need to look at appendixes or bibliographies that at times are meaningless. If you do this over time you will develop the confidence that you are a lifelong learner, and you are committed to the profession.

FINAL THOUGHTS

At the start of every school year, teachers return from vacation and walk into their classroom with anticipation of a rewarding school year. The mandates begin to swirl around, and opening-day activities update the teachers on school-wide and district-wide initiatives for the upcoming school year. Master teachers embrace these initiatives and make powerful contributions to the school community and act as teacher leaders in their discipline. The beginning of a new school year is exciting and invigorating.

To the teacher reading this book, please close your classroom door. Take a few minutes to remember that this is your students' classroom, a place that they will be engaged in wonderful learning experiences. This is their world, and you are the architect who is going to build a positive and productive culture for learning so that each child can reach his or her potential.

Successful schools are built on the foundation of successful classrooms. Please take control; do not be distracted by mandates and teacher evaluation systems. Create a world in which your students will flourish using the strategies and recommendations set forth in this text. Please reach—there is no limit to the opportunities that you can offer your students. Embrace each and every one of them and guide them along the continuum of success.

To parents, look at each new school year as an opportunity for your child to grow and flourish. Every year is a new start, thus providing your child with an unobscured view of what is to come, without boundaries. Teachers appreciate parent involvement and look forward to opportunities to build strong bonds and relationships with parents to provide each child with the optimal educational experience. Positive, ongoing communication supports the individual learning experience of each child.

Being a teacher is not a job or a career—it is a way of life.
—Randall Glading, PhD

9

PERSPECTIVES

The Principal

Dr. Charles Britton

In *The Qualities of a Master Teacher Today*, Dr. Glading captures the key attributes of highly effective educators. As a high school principal and assistant principal for fourteen years, I had the pleasure of working with hundreds of teachers. I believe this book succinctly outlines the key content knowledge, pedagogical skills, habits of mind, and dispositions possessed by successful teachers.

There is an inherent irony when it comes to teaching. If asked, "What is the easiest job in the world?" My answer is simple: "Being a teacher." There is nothing particularly difficult about teaching. Everyone has the capacity to teach something. For a classroom teacher, it would be easy to make copies of a series of worksheets, hand the worksheets out to students, collect the worksheets, place grades on the worksheets, hand the worksheets back to students, and use the grades to calculate an average for end-of-quarter, end-of-semester, and end-of-year grades.

If that is how a teacher chooses to instruct his or her students, then he or she has the easiest job in the world. However, if asked, "What is the most difficult job in the world?" My answer is also simple: "Being an effective teacher." Effective teachers understand that teaching is not about *teaching*; effective teachers understand that teaching is about *learning*.

The ability to create an environment in which every student learns at the highest level is unquestionably the most difficult job in the world. So, what is it that separates a mere teacher from an effective teacher? As Dr. Glading articulates, a teacher's ability to be reflective and form effective relationships are the two key attributes that separate mediocre teachers from exemplary teachers.

A reflective teacher is an individual who is constantly searching for opportunities to improve his or her practice by seeking and valuing feedback, engaging in lifelong learning, and taking advantage of every opportunity to grow. A reflective teacher understands that every year, every student, every lesson, every interaction with colleagues, parents, students, and community stakeholders offers an opportunity to grow, evolve, and improve.

A mediocre teacher will spend a thirty-year career teaching one year thirty times. A reflective teacher will invest the energy to improve his or her practice, and create individualized learning opportunities for each student. At the end of a thirty-year career, the reflective teacher will have had thirty unique experiences, each experience building on and improving on the last.

To be a reflective teacher, an educator must possess the ability to listen carefully, believe that there is always more to learn, and view each student as a unique and interesting puzzle. The reflective teacher understands his or her content material, captures the content material in high-quality curriculum, deploys a variety of instructional techniques to articulate the curriculum, and uses assessment to provide students meaningful guidance and feedback.

A reflective teacher understands that the interplay between curriculum, instruction, and assessment is not static, but rather a dynamic process that must cater to and be individualized for each student. By possessing a deep understanding of curriculum, instruction, and assessment, and using a reflective framework to consider the needs of each student, the effective teacher creates an environment in which the learning experience is unique for each student. No matter how challenging the student or situation, the reflective teacher is able to calibrate expectations and meet the needs of every learner.

In order to meet the needs of every student, an effective teacher possesses the ability to form meaningful relationships. Effective teachers create meaningful relationships through genuine, personal, and authentic interactions with students, parents, and colleagues. A chain is only as strong as its weakest link, and a school community is only as strong as its weakest relationship.

It takes the collective effort of the entire community to educate a student. Effective relationships must exist between and among all teachers in order to communicate needs and challenges, and collectively identify solutions to problems of practice. Effective relationships must also exist between teachers and parents. If effective relationships do not exist between teachers and parents, teachers will squander critical opportunities to extend learning from the classroom into the home. And, most importantly, effective relationships must exist between students and teachers.

Students must trust their teachers and feel that teachers care deeply about their learning and well-being. An effective teacher understands that it takes hard work and constant tending to develop and maintain effective relationships. The effective teacher recognizes when relationships are breaking down, and works proactively to mend and improve relationships.

In order to develop and maintain effective relationships with students, teachers must care deeply for each individual student and possess a wide variety of skills and content knowledge. Teachers who develop positive and productive relationships with students understand child development and learning theory, and possess the ability to motivate and inspire students. Through a balance of humor, empathy, clear communication, and trust, effective teachers use the power of effective relationships to establish high expectations and create engaging, challenging, interesting, and rigorous learning experiences.

Effective teachers understand that learning necessitates failure. Without failure, learning will not occur. With the development of effective student-teacher relationships, students learn to trust their teacher and develop a growth mind-set through which failure is expected and valued as a means to learning. Without an effective relationship, students will fear failure, develop a fixed mind-set, and either internalize failure and believe it is a reflection of their intelligence and ability, or externalize failure and blame the teacher or the content material. If you have ever heard a student say, "I'm just not good at that" or "I don't like that subject," then you've discovered a student who encountered a teacher who failed to develop an effective relationship.

The ability to be a reflective practitioner and to develop meaningful relationships are skills that have stood the test of time. However, the twenty-first-century public school classroom presents some challenges and opportunities that are unique for teachers today. Effective teachers understand how the twenty-first century is modifying the ways teachers reflect on their practice and develop positive relationships.

Today's teachers must recognize and be able to reflect on and value the fact that they are part of a vital social contract that frames the trajectory and success of our nation. Reflective teachers understand that they are government employees, and value the role that they play as a civil servant. As a civil servant, teachers are part of the democratic process and are subject to political forces at the federal, state, and local levels that maintain the very existence of public education.

Today's political process has introduced levels of accountability that make the twenty-first-century classroom unique when compared with earlier eras. Effective teachers must be able to reflect on and understand new expectations that hold teachers accountable for the success of every student. Reflective teachers do not fear accountability that comes with teacher evaluation, standardized testing, school choice, and measurements that report the efficacy of schools by publicly posting metrics such dropout rates, student and teacher attendance, types and number of school disciplinary actions, standardized test results, and other measures of school success.

Teachers who are not reflective will fear accountability, blame the political process, and allow political processes that seek to improve public schools to destroy morale and dampen their passion for teaching. Reflective teachers respect the political process, raise their voice to inform the political process, and constantly seek to find the positive aspect in every decision that frames the operation of public schools. Reflective teachers are agents of change, not obstacles.

Reflective teachers also recognize and value the fact that we are in a constantly evolving environment. New standards, technology, research, best practices, and teaching techniques are dramatically changing the twenty-first-century classroom. We have entered an era in which every student expects an individualized learning plan. The age-old factory model of public education in which seat time and Carnegie units determined student promotion is giving way to an era in which learning is the expectation and time is the variable.

Reflective teachers see the value in new approaches, are hungry to learn new pedagogical techniques, are eager to learn about and deploy new technology, and are excited to learn how new research informs the way we conceptualize student learning. Like a lawyer or a doctor who must constantly stay up to date with new practices and information, a reflective teacher is a white-collar professional who understands that he or she must stay informed, and constantly try new techniques and approaches. A reflective teacher understands that if we are not moving forward, we are falling behind.

The twenty-first century is also altering how effective teachers develop and maintain teacher-student relationships. A teacher's knowledge and ability to transmit that knowledge to students once defined student-teacher roles and framed the student-teacher relationship. Now, the ease of access to information facilitated by the Internet, social media, and omnipresent technology is redefining those traditional boundaries.

In the twenty-first-century classroom, information is literally at students' fingertips. Teachers are no longer in sole possession of information that students need in order to progress through a grade or subject. Teachers must recognize that they are no longer the authority or oracle of all information and must reconceptualize the traditional student-teacher relationship.

In today's student-teacher relationships, teachers must view themselves as facilitators rather than purveyors of knowledge. The traditional image of a teacher at the front of the classroom explaining and purveying information to students has given way to a more collaborative relationship through which teachers focus on helping students use information, rather than commit information to memory.

New expectations have also altered how teachers develop and maintain relationships with colleagues and parents. In the past, teaching was an insular profession; teachers were empowered to close their classroom doors and provide instruction independent of input from parents and colleagues.

The twenty-first-century classroom is far more transparent. Effective teachers understand that the formation of effective relationships requires educators to be open to feedback from colleagues, and they value professional learning conversations through which curriculum, instruction, and assessment practices are common and collaboration frames ongoing school improvement. Effective teachers also value and actively seek opportunities for parents to provide input into the educational process. Effective twenty-first-century parent-teacher relationships are collaborative, and parent input into the instructional process is valued.

The twenty-first-century classroom is a dynamic and evolving environment. As Dr. Glading captures in this book, effective teachers understand how the modern classroom environment is shaping and transforming how educators reflect on their practice and develop meaningful relationships. Teachers who develop the ability to critically reflect on their practice—and develop and maintain effective relationships—will serve their students well and ensure that every student is provided a high-quality academic experience that will equip learners with twenty-first-century skills, dispositions, and habits of mind.

10

PERSPECTIVES

The Teacher

Jessica Gleason

How can I improve? Am I doing enough? How can I motivate and engage my students while still offering rigorous lessons that challenge them? Are they learning? Are they improving? Was this lesson effective? Am I effective?

These are questions that constantly run through my mind as I continue my journey to becoming a master teacher.

As a veteran teacher with over a decade's worth of teaching in public schools and various other programs, I am constantly evolving to become a master teacher. From my perspective, a master teacher is one who not only possesses the TEACHERS qualities that Dr. Glading discusses in this book, but also is an individual who is constantly learning, revising, and adapting in order to meet the needs of his or her students. A master teacher must be flexible and open, welcoming and engaging, knowledgeable and caring.

TECHNIQUE

The master teacher is a master performer. As teachers, we wear a variety of hats, and these hats sometimes feel as if they're about to topple over and smother us all! Teachers not only have several roles as educators—counseling, parenting, and so forth—but they also must perform as a means to encourage and motivate learners.

To be quite honest, I find myself (as do my colleagues) exhausted and spent at the end of most days, as I have spent the past six hours "onstage," connecting with students, materials, and the world around us to try to bring learning alive for students. Think of the last concert you went to. The artist was probably drained after leaving all he had on the stage—that is how a master teacher can feel!

However, I must say that a radical shift occurred for me my first few years teaching. My experience as a student was always teacher centered. I remember row after row of desks leading to a teacher podium where a lecture spewed for forty-three minutes and I was expected to furiously scribble notes. Now, while I had a great education, it's not until I was finally asked to experiment with things and discuss my ideas in college that I feel as though I was an active participant in my own learning. Before, I listened and retained. Now, in college, I learned.

How does a master teacher, then, ensure that students learn? You must put them as the focal point. It seems obvious, but it's actually something that many teachers struggle with. Many teachers still believe they teach their content. I've heard many a teacher identify themselves as a teacher of biology, English, or American government, and while this is true, you are truly a teacher of children. You teach children English, you don't teach English to children.

Remembering this will allow for student-centered instruction that allows you to create rigorous activities that allow for higher-order thinking skills. Cooperative learning and authentic learning experiences are a must, as students must feel the relevance in their own lives. One thing that I have always prided myself on is giving activities, assignments, units a purpose. I explain to students what we are doing and why it matters. Our goals and objectives are relayed in student-friendly language that they help to create and thus, own.

EMPATHY

Students can smell phoniness. It's something in their genetic makeup that allows them to sniff out a teacher who is, in the words of Holden Caulfield, a phony. Trust me, if you do not care, they do not care. If you do not care, then please allow me to ask—why are you teaching? If you're a teacher, then you are an intelligent person with many options open—and again, in the nicest way, find an avenue that fulfills you. I hate to say it, but it is okay to not be a teacher! If you do not care, if you do not have empathy for the students, if you do not want to listen to them and focus on their needs, then it's okay to do something else, trust me!

I honestly believe that it takes a special calling, just like every other profession, and a special person to fulfill the shoes of a master teacher. These master teachers care. They can put students at the focal point of their lessons because of this compassion they have. They know their individual students and they remember them, and are remembered for it. We all remember teachers who cared—and sadly, teachers who didn't.

I myself can remember a time in fifth grade when I questioned what an A+ meant. It was the first time we received letter grades on our report cards and I had studied the key section. The teacher replied that it was the highest possible score, but one that was very hard to get. I innocently declared that I wanted to get one, and this teacher chuckled and said he did not think I could. I was beyond embarrassed and felt, frankly, stupid. He did not think I was capable? Was I not capable?

Being an incredibly stubborn individual, I worked tirelessly to earn that A+, and while some may argue that it was good motivation, I disagree. I could have earned that A+ anyway due to my work ethic and love of the subject. I do not remember him for motivating me; I remember him for embarrassing and not believing in me.

Now, I am not a Lifetime afternoon special watcher. I do not even try to say that it is easy to care. It can be difficult, challenging, and draining. There are some students who will push you away and use terrible defense mechanisms to ease their pain. But as an adult and master teacher, you must realize that these children are feeling their own pain and it is your job to help them deal with it.

Teaching in an inner-city school, I have seen the worst pain in the eyes of a rejected thirteen-year-old. I have heard parents tell me, "I'm done with him; he's your problem." That type of pain is unspeakable, and a teacher needs to remember what children go through. I always try to teach my students empathy through example. They do not know my story, I may not always know theirs, but we need to respect one another and be there for one another.

Above all, we need to pay attention. A master teacher not only cares and listens, but also pays attention. My most recent school amazed me the first week because everyone knew everyone. The teachers all knew the kids and their families and this allowed them to individualize their education and best reach their needs. Sitting on a Student Assistance Team was eye opening, as a child was referred by a teacher and adults worked together to try to think of ways to help that child. This needs to be in all schools and all teachers should have the opportunity to serve on it.

Contact home for good and bad. Master teachers are in constant contact with students and their families and report both positive and negative situations. Students are used to getting calls when they are in trouble, but calling to report about a student's improvement is a way to get that behavior to stay.

ASSESSMENT

In today's world, we are driven by data. Excel spreadsheets are created, compiled, collaborated, corroborated, calibrated . . . my mind spins with the numbers. As educators, data has always been a part of our day, but recent changes and updates to teacher evaluation have been pressure on. However, there is no need to be overwhelmed, as master teachers use this as information. A master teacher will not be intimidated by the data; rather, he will embrace it. It will change your practice if you can see it as another means to an end: helping your students succeed.

Rather than feel the pressures of numbers, help it to highlight your students' potential. I use the data from our assessments every day as it guides my lesson planning and shapes my year. I use it to understand where my students are and where they need to be. If anything, it has helped to give a purpose to my teaching and allow me to see what my students need in a clear way. Data can be used to identify students who used to go under the radar, for example, the quiet student who does okay and does not cause a fuss in class, but now we see that she struggles with this concept in algebra and must master this concept in science.

I also think we need to encourage our students to look at data. It's their performances; they should take ownership. However, this can't result in added pressure. Rather, I have my students reflect—and not just on numbers but on the feedback I give. What comments are they frequently seeing on their papers? What question stems do they frequently miss on AP multiple-choice quizzes? Noticing these trends can help them to focus on not only what they are doing well, but also areas they need to strengthen.

A master teacher will also give authentic experiences as assessment. I urge all schools to allow students to have creative, authentic experiences that they will remember their whole lives. I remember one of my colleagues was allowed to use an empty classroom for an assignment where her students brought Dante's levels of hell to life. This did not just turn into analyzing literature; they had to engineer, plan, execute designs, and collaborate with one another. Students took different roles and were incredibly self-motivated. It culminated into visits from the whole school where underclassmen excitedly asked if they would be "allowed" to read this book.

Student choice is also essential. Master teachers know what their students need but they help their students find it for themselves through choice. Allowing students to take ownership over their learning is key to creating those lifelong learners that education is all about.

CONTENT

Speaking of lifelong learners, master teachers themselves are always learning, always reflecting, and always changing. They strive to be masters of their content area and constantly are engaged in their own material. Seek out professional development and be excited about your area—if you're not, no student will be.

I will be the first to admit it—I'm no expert. And I argue that master teachers do not see themselves as experts, but rather as "fluid keepers of knowledge." They realize they must be adaptable, flexible, and ready for change. They instruct, they learn, they are a part of the process in the classroom, they are not the process.

If you want to be a master teacher, you must always be willing to learn. Being a lifelong learner is something that I pride myself on and I think something that all master teachers consider themselves.

A former colleague continuously amazed me by her repeated attendance at the same workshop each summer. When asked why she kept going back to the same conference, year after year, she replied, "Well, a year has gone by. I've learned, the presenter has learned, other attendees have learned. What we share changes and how we move forward changes as well." She knew that the collaboration from other open-minded colleagues would teach her something about herself, her content, and her instruction.

I also believe that master teachers must be citizen orators, to borrow from the College Board's language. Master teachers are aware of our global, always changing society, and make connections to it in their teaching. My current school undertook an initiative to link lessons to the United Nation's Global Goals, helping to not only authenticate our lessons but also to inspire discussion that connects with outside our classroom walls, town, state, and world. Citizens of our country need to be aware of others and connect what they're learning with what they're going to need to be doing.

HUMOR AND ENERGY

I'll never forget a physics teacher who, facing a roomful of seniors utterly baffled by the world of physics, played up an "invisible student" routine. Since no one could even formulate the vocabulary needed to ask a question, he would race to the back of the room, sit, and frantically raise his hand and ask questions. He then would run to the front of the room and answer the question. As silly as it sounds, it was entertaining and did allow for a break in the lecture.

Natural humor and energy is part of what it takes to be a master teacher. Your personality is your own—own it and translate it into teaching. Students will detect a false sense of humor and respond negatively. In the same vein, students will be unmotivated by a sense of low energy. If you are not into your lessons, why would they be?

A master teacher will harness student energy into high performance. A master teacher will also be able to use different personalities and energies for different purposes. No student is alike and no teacher will be, either, so there's no magic formula. However, positivity and honesty is key. The worst is sarcasm.

In my experience, students do not respond well to sarcasm, and most gets lost in translation. It's never "funny" to make fun of students or put them on "blast." One of the first things I tell teachers that I mentor is, "You're not their friend. You're their teacher." Humor and energy can sometimes get misconstrued into thinking that a friendship is forming. Lifelong relationships of respect and communication about future endeavors is one thing, but believing a teacher to be one's friend is another. Lines can be blurred easily and teachers must draft a staunch line to separate.

RELATIONSHIPS

That brings me to relationships. Everything discussed here leads to the relationship that you build with students. Remember that no relationships will be the same and you need to look at each as an individual.

Communication is key as a teacher. Not only do you need to be clear in your goals, assessments, activities, but also in your feedback and criticism. Criticism needs to be helpful, specific, and frequent. Rubrics are essential, but teacher-friendly ones do not help students.

Terms like *reaching* or *generally* or *limited* mean nothing to students. Rather, you need to say specifically: "You did well here; you need to work on this." It also needs to be given in a timely manner. I cannot tell you the number of times a colleague has graded an assignment collected weeks before. Students need to have the opportunity to revise. A master teacher will look at everything as a teachable moment, and that includes each assignment.

A master teacher also develops relationships with his colleagues, not just with students. Having a community that works together is always in the best interest of the student. Working with a peer or curriculum partner is important as new ideas may be discussed, norms created, and student issues noticed. I find my best work is done when I am discussing ideas aloud and someone else shares or comments. However, a school needs to create a safe community where people feel supported and able to share. If that's not happening where you are, then be the change. Start it. Find like-minded teachers and start working together. Your students will be better for it.

Students also need master teachers who are involved in their community. A product of Jesuit education myself, I believe in the power of teaching the whole individual. I am more than my academic performance and therefore must be treated as such. Students learn lessons both inside and outside of the classroom just as an athlete learns on and off the field and an actor on and off the stage. Teachers must engage in order to learn their students in a new light. Committees, extracurriculars, attending sports games all help to create an engaged master teacher who has the pulse of the school and the needs of the student in mind.

STYLE

Finally, style. Everything discussed previously leads to this and again, this is something you can't fake, you can't create, but you can finesse. Be personal, genuine, and comfortable. Do not force things and instead, enhance and refine them. I always think that the more preparation, the better. I used to think out and create outlines during some lessons because it helped my classes flow better. Do not read from a script—but actually, if it takes that the first few weeks to jump-start your journey to becoming a master teacher, then try. Try different things. Keep learning, keep trying. Observe others! That is key to all your questions!

A colleague painted the following quotation by Daniel Quinn over his whiteboard: "Teacher seeks pupil. Must have an earnest desire to save the world." It's easy to focus on the impact there of what the pupil can learn from that teacher. However, I look at it in a different way. I've always read it as a teacher needs a pupil, and a pupil needs his teacher, in order to save the world.

II

PERSPECTIVES

The Parent

Alison Rodilosso

In the course of the education of my children, there are a few teachers who have made a long-standing positive impact on their lives. These are educators who humbly embody the lofty characteristics of a master teacher, each with their own unique personality, style, and skill set that they bring into the classroom each and every day. Over the years, I have not found one foolproof formula that works to make a teacher outstanding. After all, there are so many variables involved in the education of a student, including many factors outside the control of the educator.

Nonetheless, there are certain characteristics and qualities that each teacher embodies that result in a highly effective teaching method. Some of these traits are unusual and surprising and probably would not appear in a handbook outlining typical successful strategies in the classroom. And yet they work. I am not a professional educator, nor have I been trained in the ways of school administration, so I offer only anecdotal information that highlights some of the successful experiences my children have had over the past ten years. No child is lucky enough to have only good teachers, and unfortunately, we have had our share of inadequate ones.

However, those stories are for another time. In the next few pages, I discuss the outstanding teachers my kids have had, and the qualities and skills they brought to the classroom that made them so effective.

Teaching a young student to write well is undoubtedly a difficult, often seemingly insurmountable, task. What, after all, constitutes a well-written sentence, paragraph, or book? Learning grammar rules can certainly help guide a writer to craft organized, clear thoughts; however, this only begins to scratch the surface. In fact, many of the best writers often break or disregard the rules.

Many complex skills such as style, vocabulary, voice, perspective, and clarity are all critical to determining the quality of a piece of writing. These more abstract concepts are very difficult, if not impossible, to teach, thus the quagmire facing composition instructors. Nonetheless, certain teachers find a way to break through to their students.

My two daughters were fortunate to have an instructor their freshman year of high school who knew how to teach the art of writing. Mr. Thurman taught in an unconventional but highly effective manner. He was able to keep their attention throughout class while properly instructing and inspiring them. Mr. Thurman taught three courses: AP Language and Composition, satire, and a ninth-grade composition course.

He possessed a very strong personality and was very direct with all the students. He never sugarcoated his feedback and let them know when their work was subpar and in need of vast improvement. There was no dancing around the truth. If a student offered an answer in class that he considered inferior, he let them know it. He would not mince his words and let the students get away with work that was lazy, thoughtless, or poorly written. This approach may seem off putting, and perhaps at times it was, but, the end result was highly motivated students who paid attention in class, learned to write well, and never wanted to disappoint Mr. Thurman.

His slights never cut to the core, but instead the students generally found them humorous. He somehow managed to draw the students in, rather than offending them and pushing them away. The fear of disappointing their teacher made many of the students work harder to become stronger writers, and some even excelled. He insisted that his students' work possess an academic rigor heretofore unexplored by most. Mr. Thurman understood that because writing well is so difficult, and communication can often be murky, his critique had to be clear and break through the clutter. His directness proved effective.

Mr. Thurman was not a bully whose goal was to embarrass the students, and he never picked on anyone. He treated everyone the same—no one was spared his commentary—and this approach unified the class. He understood how to walk the line between providing clear, constructive feedback and discouraging critiques.

In addition to possessing a formidable personality, Mr. Thurman was very knowledgeable about the process of writing and had a vast understanding of literature and world events. He alternated assignments: at times he encouraged the students to write about topics of interest to them, and other times he assigned themes to challenge the students. He often led discussions centering on current or historical events about which he wanted the students to know and write.

He insisted that their writing be relevant, and he always encouraged the students to develop their own style and voice. Mr. Thurman would often tell stories about his own life—some were funny, some weird, and some poignant—to provide students with examples of how to tell an interesting story. He wanted his students to understand that whether discussing world events or personal experiences, the importance of writing well remains paramount. There was never a dull moment in Mr. Thurman's class, and my daughters always looked forward to attending. It was not a class for napping, but one for participating and learning. Classes were lively and discussion oriented. He did not simply read facts and figures off a PowerPoint presentation, but led meaningful class discussions. He was often available to meet with students during the school day or after school to discuss their essays, and his feedback was invaluable.

Another standout teacher that one of my daughters had was Mr. McFarland for AP European History. He also taught global history. Mr. McFarland was a legend at the school, and all the students wanted to be in his section of AP European History, despite knowing the demands he placed on his students. He was an incredibly engaging lecturer whose knowledge of U.S. and world history was impressive. He could authoritatively speak on numerous topics and provide extensive answers to seemingly any question, including references to other regions of the world or other important issues of the era in question. The enthusiasm he exuded made it evident that he enjoyed his job, and his joy was infectious and motivating.

Mr. McFarland raised the bar and pushed the students to use higher-order thinking skills when they wrote their papers, spoke in class, and sat for exams. He insisted that their work be of the highest quality and infused the classroom with high energy. He sought to tap potential in all of the students by encouraging them, and he enjoyed hearing about their interests outside the classroom.

He listened to what the students had to say and responded accordingly. He organized the classroom so that the desks were arranged in a circle to facilitate communication, and he would randomly call on students to participate in the discussion. This interaction ensured that the students were well prepared for class, and not just hiding in the back of a lecture hall.

Mr. McFarland assigned extensive reading and note taking on chapters in the textbook, but these assignments were not completed in vain. Each day the class reviewed the subject matter, and Mr. McFarland explained the occurrences of the time to be certain that everyone understood the material. The students were not just teaching themselves, as Mr. McFarland took time in class to clarify the chapters of the text. Homework was always linked to his in-class discussions and, in turn, was connected to the tests he administered.

Thus, the notes were critical to success in both class participation and exam performance. By the end of the school year, each of his students had about two extensive spiral notebooks full of essential notes. These notes were considered solid gold as they were laboriously written and highly valued.

Mr. McFarland knew that many of his students had high aspirations, as virtually all the students in his AP European History class would go on to graduate from high school and attend four-year colleges, and, some would eventually enroll in graduate school. The students were encouraged to pursue their academic interests and to set their sights high. He thoroughly prepared the students for the rigorous AP European History exam at the end of the year, and many of his students did very well, achieving a perfect score of "5."

Given Mr. McFarland's expertise in his subject area, he was easily able to teach outside the syllabus by referencing other relevant historical events and time periods. He made history come alive in the classroom. When quoting a historical figure, he would adapt the voice of a character and would create hand gestures that person might have used.

This engaging form of instruction helped the students to visualize the era and see things from that person's perspective.

It was never an easy task, but Mr. McFarland required his students to examine historical events thoughtfully and critically. He often had students take conflicting points of view into consideration and then synthesize the different perspectives to develop solutions.

Mr. McFarland also had the students personify different individuals from the various time periods and places they were studying. Each student was assigned a historical figure, and whether or not they agreed with the personality, views, and temperament, they were required to represent accurately that person for one or two days in the classroom. This requirement made for animated and imaginative conversations.

He also had the students form groups and make up songs about select time periods and present them to the class. In another assignment, he asked the students to analyze relevant art and discuss it together. This particular practice was very pertinent, as art questions often appeared on the final AP exam. At the same time, it was another way to keep the class curious and focused. Many high school students find history to be boring and irrelevant, but put the subject matter in the right hands, and suddenly the coursework is engrossing.

Mr. McFarland designed his exams in two parts over two days, with multiple choice on day one, and a series of essays on day two. This approach proved helpful to the students as it gave them focused exposure to two test-taking formats: if they were not particularly strong at negotiating multiple choice, at least they were given a chance to answer essays the following day. The questions were never easy, but the students considered them fair.

In the end, the students were all pleased that they enrolled in the class as evidenced by how popular it was year after year. With his wit, intelligence, creative teaching style, and infectious energy, Mr. McFarland was an outstanding teacher who inspired his students to excel and develop a lifelong love of learning.

Most young children are born with an innately inquisitive nature. Yet, they commence their formal early education with a combination of mixed feelings: enthusiasm, curiosity, excitement, and apprehension. And with this concoction of emotions, they land on the doorstep of a school. Fortunately, my children were lucky enough to attend an elementary school that was welcoming and encouraging. Within its hallways there were several wonderful teachers adept at nurturing and educating the students.

One of my son's first-grade teachers, Ms. Gordon, stood out as a true educator. She created an atmosphere in the classroom that allowed the children to investigate, create, explore, and organize. Her projects were imaginative and permitted the children to devise their own solutions, rather than simply coloring in between the lines or connecting the dots. The tasks had a purpose and were implemented within finite time periods, thus enabling the children to begin to learn the necessity of completing work on time.

The projects also presented an excellent opportunity for the children to learn to respect others and to share, as the crayons, scissors, and other materials were placed in the center of the table. My son, though not artistically inclined, frequently brought home very colorful, dramatic projects that demonstrated initiative and exploration, and he would eagerly explain how he created the work.

More impressive was the mood one encountered in the classroom. Whenever I walked into the room, I was struck by a sense of both calm and, perhaps contradictorily, excitement. The children seemed happy to be there and went about their activities with a studied determination. They were eager to ask questions and quickly raised their hands. There were so many imaginative answers. And when an answer was "wrong," Ms. Gordon did not embarrass the child who offered the creative response, nor was she a pushover, accepting of any reply. Instead, she found a way to convey that the correct response was an alternative not yet uttered.

Ms. Gordon was not wishy-washy; she spoke clearly, if softly, and informed the students that there are right and wrong answers and that the class was in pursuit of the right ones. She encouraged the students not to dismay, but to persevere. Whether the task was answering questions about the plot in a story, learning to spell a word, or gluing together pieces of a project, she helped the children tackle the obstacles in front of them. Given that there were twenty children in the classroom with varying degrees of interest and ability, this was no easy feat.

Through their participation, the children were learning how to solve problems, at times on their own, or occasionally, with the assistance of another child, the teacher, or the teacher's aide. Their risk taking was rewarded with praise, their motivation fueled, and their puzzle-solving ability enhanced. Hopefully these are skills that will remain with the students for the duration of their lives.

Additionally, Ms. Gordon did not tolerate any bullying or mean behavior toward other children in the classroom. From time to time this type of behavior would erupt, but she was quick to respond and kept an eye out for future indiscretions. She had a true, seemingly innate, desire for the children to be comfortable and happy in her classroom and wanted the children's confidence to grow.

She encouraged their questions and laughed along at the humorous events of the day. To keep things interesting, there were numerous special occasions that the children relished: Mystery Reader, plays, author visits, parties, mini scientific investigations, and creative art projects. Each of these initiatives proposed fresh challenges to the children and made the days pass quickly. Ms. Gordon encouraged parent participation, but with structured, specific goals.

Parents were not permitted to dictate the agenda, but they played a role in the students' learning. Homework was directly tied to the lesson taught each day and was not overwhelming for the students. Technology was incorporated through the use of computers, but it did not dominate lessons. Instead, Ms. Gordon focused on developing traits needed for future success and creating lifelong learners: initiative, creativity, curiosity, perseverance, and confidence. Ms. Gordon was steadfast in fostering these qualities even as the curriculum pendulum swung from one extreme to another.

The last teacher who really stood out from the crowd was my son and daughter's seventh-grade English teacher. Mr. Newton was the definition of the teacher who went above and beyond the call of duty. He was completely involved with his students both inside and outside the classroom.

Each Wednesday morning, he invited his students to walk with him to school from Starbucks chatting about the topics of the day. He also hosted a dinner at a local restaurant simply for the purpose of getting to know his students better. He was the teacher advisor for the middle school yearbook and was frequently seen around the school snapping photos. Within the community, he helped organize clothing drives and volunteered his time to various organizations.

While in the classroom, Mr. Newton was always positive and encouraged the students to read as much as possible. The texts he assigned were interesting, and when the students submitted their writing samples, he extensively edited the work. He taught the students how to write clear, structured paragraphs by employing a technique known as "TEXAS"-style paragraphs. From this base of knowledge, the students were able to write factual essays supported by quotes and relevant research.

Another interesting project offered an opportunity for the students to undertake an independent investigation. Having read a nonfiction book about a rescue at sea, my son interviewed a former member of the Coast Guard and visited a local Coast Guard office. The coursework also centered around reading fiction, and the assignments related to the reading were inventive. For example, the students were required to create an imaginary television interview with characters from a book revealing the story line and plot twists along the way. All these opportunities allowed the students to learn about the world while sharpening their writing skills.

Mr. Newton communicated directly with the students and ultimately held them accountable for their homework, but he also understood the importance of informing parents of upcoming due dates. To this end, he e-mailed parents daily, notifying them of forthcoming assignments. The parents were prepared lest a student declare, "I have no homework tonight." He even distributed large paper calendars so that the students could plan and organize their work.

Mr. Newton taught the students to write well, but he also insisted that they manage their time well. He knew that the students would be stronger writers and the work would be of a much higher quality if the students invested the time to reread and rewrite their assignments.

Each of the teachers I profiled possesses a very different personality and teaching style, but each person is equally effective. They honed their skills over the course of numerous years of instruction and fine-tuned their methods. Two of the teachers are high school instructors, one teaches middle school, and the fourth currently instructs first grade.

But the common thread is that all four of the teachers are very dedicated to their profession and to ensuring that their students receive the best possible instruction in their class. I am thankful that my children were enrolled in their classes and that they were given such a thorough education. They learned more than just facts and figures.

Every day they interacted with professionals who were willing to go beyond the minimal job requirements and teach valuable life lessons. I hope these principles stay with them as they embark on their own professions.

12

PERSPECTIVES

The Therapist

Amy Bernstein

Firstly, I want to thank the author for allowing me the perspective of "the therapist." I have an undergraduate degree in social work and I am proud to say that I also have a master's degree in elementary education. Therefore, I think I really understand teachers. One thing I know for sure is that we as a culture certainly ask a great deal from our modern teachers.

They are called upon to transmit traditional academics, athletics, arts, and technology, all while being experts, qualifiers, and quantifiers, as well as limitless, empathetic, and funny model citizens. A tall order for any human. I come from a family with many generations of teachers. I am proud to write that my mother-in-law was a New York City teacher and I am a product of the New York City public school system. One of the main reasons I chose to suspend my social work career after my BSW and before my MSW was because I felt a void that I thought I could fix by being an elementary school teacher.

You see, when I was just five years old, my sister, who is ten years my senior, became mentally ill. In the 1960s, people with mental illness often spent a long time in hospitals. My parents decided that they needed me to go to school full-time so they could cope with my sister's care. Therefore, my parents had me skip kindergarten and go straight to first grade.

That first-grade year for me was a disaster. Not only was my home life chaotic, but I suffered with a spelling disability. We took two weekly tests in first grade: a pretest at the beginning of the week and a spelling test at the end of the week.

Back then, teachers did not consider technique or individual learning styles. There were few and rigid methods to learning and none were the best fit for me. Luckily the teachers of today have far greater resources to utilize and have countless innovative strategies to employ when faced with bumps in the road. The bumps in the road are the opportunities for the "master" teacher to provide the content to the student in a way that makes learning possible.

Another unfortunate reality of my primary learning experience was that not one of my six teachers made it through the full year of teaching. Either there was illness or marriage or a move that took the routine of consistency away from my experience. This feeling of inconsistency painted my memory of my early educational experience, and influenced me to study elementary education. I wanted to provide the constant presence of a teacher to others that I did not receive.

Dr. Glading is a neighbor of mine, and we met when my youngest daughter and his son were a grade apart in elementary school. Our children were fast friends and although they were not attending the same school, they had many of the same experiences. I have one personal experience with our children worth sharing. Both families had retrievers. Dr. Glading's dog was named Striker and our dog was named Joy. Both were sick, and they died on the same exact day. I remember seeing Randall the day after, and we both looked at each other in a daze. But the kids had to go off to school. I'm sure those teachers took extra care of our kids on their day of loss and used this as a teachable moment. A master teacher would utilize the relationships (child development), technique (teachable moments), and empathy (love) to teach the entire classroom.

Teaching is a profession that is under transformative times. The world is an ever-changing place, and education in the United States is no exception. What we are asking of our teachers and educational staff is particularly under a microscope with the input of "Common Core." This topic is often discussed by candidates on the race to the White House. After having read the third chapter on assessment, I know that teachers today are under a great deal of pressure to teach to the test for their evaluation and for their school as a whole get the rating that is expected of it.

One teacher who was a patient of mine suffered terribly with anxiety from the pressure she felt as a teacher in a school district that demanded high-achieving students from her, despite the diverse learners she had in her classroom. She felt that her creativity was being taken away from her as a professional and that she had no autonomy. She struggled with teaching students what's good for the test scores versus what will develop them into lovers of learning.

I worked with her to help her find the balance. Many parents have recently banded together and have chosen to opt out of tests, which, for many students, has relieved a great deal of personal anxiety. Other parents have opted out as a way to protest the changes that they don't like in the educational system that their own tax dollars support. Parents often feel powerless in the school decisions regardless of whether they are involved or not.

I have been in private practice for more than twenty years. Although my practice is primarily adults, I at all given times work with children and adolescents. I worked when the Twin Towers came down, when the Sandy Hook tragedy occurred, and when, in my idyllic community, a man murdered his wife and their two children before killing himself. All three of these horrific events impacted my work personally and my community at large.

When 9/11 happened, we New Yorkers felt the tragedy a little bit too close to home. While our country had to take off its rose-colored glasses to realize that our safety was no longer what we had thought it to be, our local schools had to deal with knowing someone directly or indirectly who personally suffered a loss. The schools were riddled with grief, and the teachers had many pedagogically challenging issues on their hands. The teachers had to assure their students that, although tragedy happens, their world is still a safe place.

I know for many of the teachers that I have as clients, the days, weeks, months, and years following 9/11 were difficult times, but were nonetheless times to enhance their techniques and utilize resources that were not previously available to them. Recently, one teacher that I work with who teaches sixth- through eighth-grade social studies was confronted by a parent who didn't want her daughter to go on the 9/11

Museum field trip, as she felt the content was too much for her young daughter.

The teacher certainly understood this mother's point of view and reassured the mother that her opinion was valid and that her daughter could opt out. She also reassured the mother that teaching about 9/11 was handled in the classroom with empathy and the maturational development of all her students in mind.

The Sandy Hook tragedy brought into my practice two examples of trauma. One was a parent of a student in the school who was not directly harmed by the shooter. The parent was obviously upset and needed a place to process what he/she had to do to keep his/her child engaged in school. The resources provided to the teachers of Sandy Hook were the best that our country has to offer. I cannot imagine what it took for those teachers to resume their roles and carry on. I imagine that, for many of the teachers, the memory of their lost colleagues motivated them to carry on.

The second client of mine that came to me after Sandy Hook was a young parent of a student at the school who could not get out of his/her head the notion that "it could have been [his/her] child." We talked for a long time about his/her discomfort and angst about the lack of security in his/her child's school and the country at large. Through our work together he/she agreed to spearhead a committee in his/her school to investigate and change the safety protocols in his/her school district.

The third tragedy that I mentioned before, the murder-suicide that took place in my idyllic community in 2011, was the one that hit the closest to home. I was working with a child who was a classmate of one of the children who was murdered. This child talked openly about what the school and his/her teacher were doing to honor the two children lost. There were trees planted, gardens sowed, benches donated with memorial plaques, and services held to honor these young innocent children who were lost. The schools in our community were given the task of teaching a cruel reality.

I was amazed how the teachers in the community, who might not have been so comfortable with death, let alone a tragic death, handled this. We each handle death in our own ways and our own style. I must say that the teachers who were asked to handle this tragedy rose to the occasion with such empathy and authenticity that I know has left a lifelong impression on countless students.

I want to share a most powerful vignette of a master teacher's impact. I had been working with a middle school student who was a transgendered child. For the sake of privacy, I will not reveal the sex. This middle school child knew that he/she was not born into the anatomical body that he/she identified as. So life was very difficult in his/her early years. There were many labels attached to this young student as he/she entered school: defiant, oppositional, angry, depressed, anxiety ridden, ADD/ADHD, aggressive, sad, disruptive, stubborn, learning disabled, emotionally disabled, and on and on. In the seventh grade, this student felt safe enough to come out to his/her openly gay teacher. It was only then that life finally began to seem tolerable.

This master teacher had the personal life experience to see that this child was in horrific pain and made it possible for the student to get what he/she needed. The child was sent to another school where her/his identity was not perceived as one other than what he/she displayed. All the labels that haunted her/him were one by one quickly removed. He/she was no longer angry. He/she was no longer emotionally or academically disabled in any marked way. Today, he/she has graduated from high school and attends college.

Through the years that we worked together, he/she often would speak about how being in a new environment, with new students and teachers that only knew him/her as the human that he/she identified as, made going to school possible. He/she often spoke about the relationship that was formed with the seventh-grade teacher who shuttled him/her from a failing, unhappy and angry person to one who was able to find an environment that made sense to him/her and saved his/her life. Not only was he/she able to breathe in his/her new learning environment, he/she was able to thrive.

Another beautiful story worth sharing on behalf of all teachers is about a young second-grade student who came into my therapy practice as result of bullying. This child was the only child of a single parent. The parent fell on hard times and was forced to live with his/her elderly parents in an affluent community. This happened to be the community the parent grew up in, and therefore the child was a student at the same elementary school that the parent had attended.

It had been brought to the parent's attention that his/her child was being picked on by other students. Now, second grade is not an easy grade as social cues are often misconstrued. Nonetheless, the teacher had witnessed a couple of instances that needed her interventions. The teacher called home and spoke with my patient's parent, assuring him/ her that the teacher was also going to be calling the bully's parents.

Ultimately, the bullying subsided and a relationship was formed between the teacher and my patient's parent that allowed this parent to get involved in the school by becoming a class parent (yes, they still do exist!). This master teacher saw that this family system was in a difficult way and opened up the classroom to enable positive change. Teachers don't only teach to the children; often it is the extended family where many life lessons are learned.

How do teachers teach that you can make lemonade out of lemons? I have so many more examples where students were disappointed and teachers were essential in teaching important life lessons. The time the mediocre singer didn't get into the school play. When one of the top students in the senior class didn't get into her early decision choice. When the alternative high school only had thirty spots for students and my patient was rejected. It's the teacher who gets to demonstrate how coping is essential for a successful life.

We all are faced with disappointment. Some more than others, and what seems like a disaster to one isn't necessarily worth a bad day to another. Clearly, to me the role of the teacher in our society has grown considerably over the past twenty years since I have been in practice. The boundaries are blurred as we ask our teachers not only to teach us, but to show us the way to learn.

In many ways, I strive as a therapist to be a master teacher as well. When patients enter my office, I first work to understand their individual experiences. Then, I use the resources and tools that I have to support them emotionally. I also give my patients an emotional education, so they may implement solid coping strategies on their own. At its core, I believe that this is the same process that a master teacher uses.

A master teacher first works to understand each individual student's learning capacities. The teacher then uses the resources he or she has to teach the students in the way that is best for each one to learn. Finally, in addition to imparting information to the students, the teacher imbues the children with an understanding of *how* to learn, hopefully creating a lover of learning. I hope you all will use this book to create students who love learning. Good luck.

REFERENCES

Anderson, L. (2001). http://epltt.coe.uga.edu/index.php?title=Bloom's_Taxonomy

Bloom, B. (1956). https://cft.vanderbilt.edu/guides-sub-pages/blooms-taxonomy/

Cruz, B. C., & Patterson, J. (2005). Cross-cultural simulations in teacher education: Developing empathy and understanding. *Multicultural Perspectives*, 7(2), 40–47. ISSN: 1521-0960.

Clinton, Hillary Rodham. *It Takes a Village: And Other Lessons Children Teach Us.* New York: Simon & Schuster, 1996. Print.

The Common Core State Standards. www.corestandards.org/ELA-Literacy.

Danielson, C. (2014). *Enhancing professional practice: A framework for teaching* (2nd ed.). Alexandria, VA: Association for Supervision and Curriculum Development.

Freedom Writers. Paramount Home Entertainment, 2007.

Freire, P. (1997). *Pedagogy of hope: Reliving pedagogy of the oppressed.* (Robert R. Barr, Trans.; with notes by Ana Maria Araujo Freire.) New York, NY: Continuum.

Friedman, Thomas L. *The World Is Flat: A Brief History of the Twenty-first Century.* New York: Farrar, Straus and Giroux, 2005. Print.

Glading, R. (2008). *Overcoming the senior slump: Meeting the challenge with internships.* Lanham, MD: Rowman & Littlefield.

Glasser, W. (1999). *The quality school: Managing students without coercion* (3rd ed.). New York, NY: HarperCollins.

Good Will Hunting. Miramax Films, 1997.

Higgins-D'Alessandro, A. (2002). The necessity of teacher development. *New Directions for Child and Adolescent Development [serial online]*, 98, 75–83. Available from: ERIC, Ipswich, MA. Accessed October 2, 2016.

Hunter, M. (1989). Madeline Hunter in the English classroom. *English Journal*, 78(5), 16. doi:10.2307/819193

Ikwumelu, S. N., Oyibe, O. A., & Oketa, E. C. (2015). Adaptive teaching: An invaluable pedagogic practice in social studies education. *Journal of Education and Practice*, 6(33), 140–144. ISSN: 2222-1735.

International Center for Leadership in Education. (2016). The Rigor/Relevance Framework. Retrieved from www.leadered.com/our-philosophy/rigor-relevance-framework.php

Karadag, R. (2010). Teachers' efficacy perceptions about individualized instruction. *International Journal of the Humanities, 8.* ISSN: 1447-9508.

Karate Kid. 1984.

Marshall, K. (2013). *Rethinking teacher supervision and evaluation: How to work smart, build collaboration, and close the achievement gap* (2nd ed.). San Francisco, CA: Wiley.

Mester, D., Spruill, S., Giani, J., Morote, E., & Inserra, A. (2015). Personal safety and teacher/student relationships viewed through black/white framework in a suburban middle school: An exploratory study. *Journal for Leadership and Instruction [serial online]*, *14*(1), 15–19. Available from: ERIC, Ipswich, MA. Accessed October 2, 2016.

Meyers, C., Molefe, A., & Brandt, C. (2015). The impact of the "Enhancing Missouri's Instructional Networked Teaching Strategies" (eMINTS) program on student achievement, 21st-century skills, and academic engagement—Second-year results. *Society for Research on Educational Effectiveness [serial online]*. Available from: ERIC, Ipswich, MA. Accessed October 2, 2016.

Peck, M. S. (2003). *The road less traveled: A new psychology of love, traditional values, and spiritual growth* (25th ed.). New York, NY: Simon & Schuster.

Säfström, C. (2014). The passion of teaching at the border of order. *Asia-Pacific Journal of Teacher Education [serial online]*, *42*(4), 337–346. Available from: ERIC, Ipswich, MA. Accessed October 2, 2016.

Saving Private Ryan. Dir. Steven Spielberg. Prod. Steven Spielberg. By Robert Rodat. Perf. Tom Hanks, Edward Burns, and Tom Sizemore. DreamWorks Pictures. 1998.

Shing, C., Saat, R., & Loke, S. (2015). The knowledge of teaching—Pedagogical content knowledge (PCK). *Malaysian Online Journal of Educational Sciences [serial online]*, *3*(3), 40–55. Available from: ERIC, Ipswich, MA. Accessed October 2, 2016.

Stevenson, M. (1939). Footprints in the sand. Retrieved from http://www.footprints-inthe-sand.com/index.php?page=Poem/Poem.php

Strean, W. (2008). Evolving toward laughter in learning. *Collected Essays on Learning and Teaching [serial online]*, *1*, 75–79. Available from: ERIC, Ipswich, MA. Accessed October 2, 2016.

To Sir with Love. Prod. James Clavell, John R. Sloan, Tony Woollard, Ian Whittaker, John Wilson-Apperson, Jill Carpenter, and Betty Glasow. By James Clavell, Ron Grainer, Philip Martell, Paul Beeson, Peter Thornton, Dino Di Campo, Bert Ross, and Ted Karnon. Dir. James Clavell. Perf. Sidney Poitier, Christian Roberts, Judy Geeson, Suzy Kendall, Ann Bell, Faith Brook, Geoffrey Bayldon, Christopher Chittell, Adrienne Posta, Lynn Sue Moon, Anthony Villaroel, and Lulu. Columbia Pictures Corp. Presents, 1967.

Turner, S. (2014). Creating an assessment-centered classroom: Five essential assessment strategies to support middle grades student learning and achievement. *Middle School Journal (J3) [serial online]*, *45*(5), 3–16. Available from: ERIC, Ipswich, MA. Accessed October 2, 2016.

Webster's New Twentieth Century Dictionary, 2nd edition, 1983.

Wimbrow, Dale. (1934). The guy in the glass. Retrieved from www.theguyintheglass.com/gig.htm

ABOUT THE AUTHOR

Dr. **Randall Glading** worked in public education for thirty-five years. He is currently the department chair and professor in the Educational Leadership and Literacy Department at Sacred Heart University in Fairfield, Connecticut. He is committed to informing parents, teachers, and all members of the school community of the evolution of teaching. The book highlights the qualities of a master teacher in today's schools.